THE fonDUE cookbook

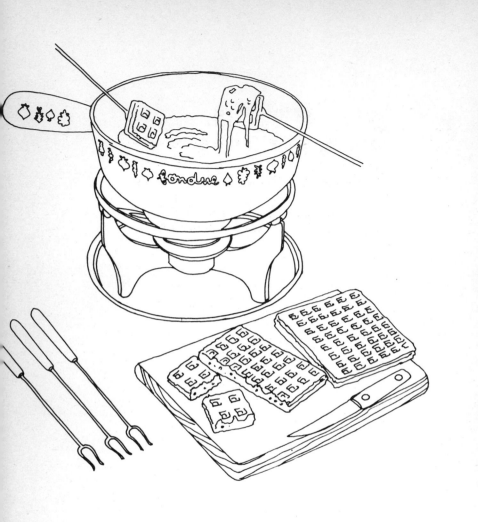

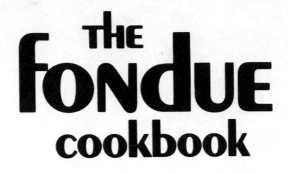

THE fONdUE cookbook

Compiled ANd EdiTEd
by bETH MERRiMAN

Published in Association with *Parade Magazine*

Cover photo courtesy Mazola Corn Oil

GROSSET & DUNLAP
Publishers   *New York*

Acknowledgements

Acknowledgement is gratefully made to the following sources for recipes published in this book. The recipes are identified by the alphabetical symbols shown at the left.

A   Adolph's Ltd
AC   Ac'cent International
AD   American Dairy Association
AR   Armour and Co.
BB   Grocery Store Products (B in B Mushrooms)
BF   Best Foods, Division Corn Products Co.
C   Campbell Soup Co.
CC   California Canners and Growers (Diet Delight Foods)
D   Del Monte Corp.
F   The RT French Co. Test Kitchens
G   General Foods Kitchens
H   H.J. Heinz Co.
HW   Hunt Wesson Kitchens
IM   International Milling Co.
IS   International Shrimp Council
K   Kraft Kitchens
LF   Lawrey's Foods, Inc.
LL   Land O'Lakes Creameries, Inc.
LM   Libby, McNeill and Libby
N   Nestlé Test Kitchens
ND   National Dairy Council
P   Poultry and Egg National Board
Q   The Quaker Oats Co.
R   Van Camp Sea Food Co. Division of
          Ralston-Purina Co.
S   Swift and Co.
ST   Standard Brands Inc. (Fleischmann's Yeast)
T   McIlhenny Co. (Tabasco)
TL   Thomas J. Lipton, Inc.
U   Wm. Underwood Co.

Contents

Introduction

Fondue parties grow more popular with every passing moment. Some hostesses specialize in cheese fondue, others prefer fondue Bourguignonne while the more adventuresome try their hand at both.

In this book you will find the traditional recipes augmented with a great variety of adaptations. There is even a special recipe for campers, made with ingredients that emerge from cans and packages! Something for everyone.

BETH MERRIMAN

THE fonDue
cookbook

1. Fondue Equipment

It's everywhere. In the housewares sections of department stores, in specialty shops like Hammacher Schlemmer in New York City, and in mail order houses. And the price range is wide. You can buy a fondue pot in a wrought iron stand on a copper or stainless steel tray for around $16.00 (department store). Or a ceramic pot, four 4-sectioned ceramic plates, four stainless steel forks with rosewood handles, a brass finish stand over an alcohol burner and an asbestos table mat for $18.95 (mail order house).

Then there is a 2-quart enamelled aluminum double pot with black bakelite handles, in avocado, orange or yellow, for $12.00 (department store).

A 2-quart copper fondue set on a 9-inch copper-plated tray with rosewood handles and an alcohol burner sells for $20.00 (department store).

A 2-quart chafing dish in copper or brass with a tin lining, made in Portugal, and having wooden handles and an alcohol burner costs $25.00 (department store).

An enamel-on-steel fondue pot imported from Norway

sells for about $25.00 (department store).

A 1 ½-quart stainless steel fondue cooker with a stainless steel warming stand and tray costs around $30.00 (department store).

Earthenware dish (left) for cheese fondue; enameled steel pot (center) for beef fondue; deep, earthenware dish with warming candle (right) for chocolate fondue

In specialty shops prices range from $25.00 for a fondue pot to $100.00 for an elaborate set that includes compartmented plates, a large tray, forks, and bowls for sauces.

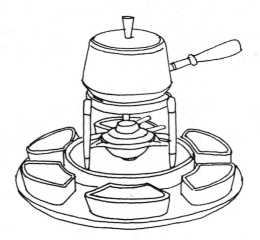

Fondue set

Fork sets (6) with rosewood handles, some with a stand, begin at $5.00. With a wooden gift box, the price may be a little higher.

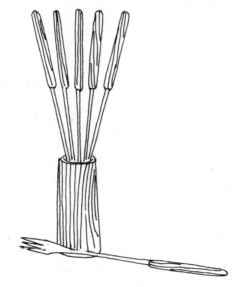

Rosewood fork set

Compartmented plates, a little larger than the usual salad plate are sold in sets of four, and the price range is wide, depending on the quality and design of the china.

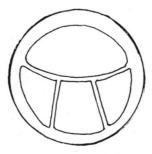

Compartmented plate

A set of forks or plates makes a welcome hostess gift, while a fondue pot at whatever price you wish to pay, would be a good choice for a wedding or shower gift.

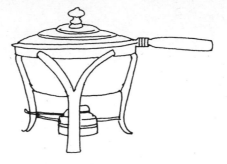

Chafing dish

Heaters for Fondues

Alcohol Burners

Some fondue stands are equipped with an alcohol burner that has a wick. Heat can be regulated by lengthening or shortening the wick, or if it is a compressed fiber wick, by opening or closing the damper.

The fuel is usually denatured alcohol although rubbing alcohol can be used. Denatured alcohol heats much more rapidly and is better for cooking. Rubbing alcohol is best for keeping foods hot. NEVER ADD FUEL UNTIL FLAME IS COMPLETELY OUT.

Canned Heat

Canned heat (Sterno) is sold in units with a stand and a holder for the canned heat. The holder has a handle which is used to regulate the flame. Some units hold a large can (7 ounces) which will burn for 4 to 5 hours. Most units are designed for a small can (2 ⅛ ounces) which burns 55 to 65 minutes.

Candles

Casseroles are often equipped with a stand which includes a candle holder. Any fireproof casserole or pot can be used on such a stand. Candles will keep food hot, but the heat is not intense enough for cooking.

Electric Skillets

The buffet-style electric skillet is increasingly popular because it is good looking enough to bring to the table and because it has a good heat control to regulate the heat and hold it steady.

2. Cheese Fondue

Presumably the noun fondue came from the French verb *fondre,* meaning "to melt," because cheese fondue is a dish of melted cheese and wine.

Nowadays Switzerland is a modern, prosperous country and poverty is practically nonexistent, but many years ago, before modern improvements became a part of life on the farm, things were a bit different. Cheese fondue had its origin in necessity.

In those old days cheese and bread were made during the summer and fall and had to last the year round. Both usually hardened to the point of being inedible. Bread, of course, could be dunked in milk, coffee, tea or wine to soften it. Cheese was melted down, placed in the center of the scrubbed wooden kitchen table and used as a "dunk" for the broken pieces of hard bread.

Today a more elaborate version of this dunk, made with cheese, wine, liqueur and seasonings, is called Cheese Fondue and is considered haute cuisine by epicures when properly made. It is an ideal dish for a light luncheon or supper or for a late evening snack.

Experts tell us that the Swiss cheese used in fondue must be well-aged or the fondue will be stringy and lumpy. In Switzerland the minimum aging period is four months and may extend to ten months. The two types of cheese used in fondue are Emmentaler (or Emmenthaler) and Gruyère. Emmentaler is milder, with larger holes, and the rind is smooth and amber colored. Gruyère has tiny holes and the rind is brown and wrinkled.

Fondues of mildest flavor are made with Emmentaler cheese alone. For stronger flavor, half Emmentaler and half Gruyère. Well-aged Gruyère alone makes fondue of strongest flavor.

It is best to cut the cheese into very small pieces, or if you're in a hurry, it may be shredded. In these forms it melts more smoothly than when it is grated.

The type of wine used in making cheese fondue is important. It should be a light, lively, dry white wine such as Neuchâtel, Rhine, Riesling or Chablis. If the wine is not tart enough it may be necessary to add a little lemon juice, about 1 ½ teaspons for every half pound of cheese.

Kirsch (cherry brandy) is the liqueur preferred by the Swiss in making fondue, but brandy cognac, light white rum or applejack may be used or the liqueur may be omitted entirely. French bread for dunking should be crusty so that the tines of the fondue fork can hold it firmly. It is best to buy small loaves and cut it so that each piece has crust on two sides. This is important, because if a piece of bread is dropped off the fork the owner must pay a forfeit! If the culprit is a man he must either "pay for the whole works" or for the next bottle of wine, depending on the mood of the guests. If it is a girl, she must kiss her male companion, or whatever man happens to be beside her at the table. Sometimes the unlucky one is required to sing a song, do a trick, or otherwise make himself a figure of fun. No wonder the Swiss say "Fondue tastes good and fosters a happy, gay atmosphere." No wonder it was a favorite of King Edward VII when he was a merry-making Prince of Wales!

The great gastronome, Brillat-Savarin, originated a dish

which he called "fondue" but which was really creamy scrambled eggs with a small amount of Gruyère cheese, butter and seasonings. In France today this is what you will get if you ask for fondue.

Fondue al' Italienne is really soufflé, "baked" over hot water for as long as 1 ½ to 2 hours, until it is firm enough to turn out on a serving dish.

But genuine Swiss cheese fondue is our main interest, after all and we shall see that making it requires patience plus the right equipment, as well as the correct ingredients.

Cooking begins by heating the wine over direct low heat until air bubbles form (this must not be confused with boiling—wine should never be boiled). Then the cheese is added, a "handful" (about ½ cup) at a time, while stirring. Some experts say the stirring must be done with a silver fork, others recommend a wooden spoon. Some say stir round and round, some say stir in the shape of a figure eight. We say, just keep stirring, making sure each batch of cheese is melted before adding the next. Next the seasoning—salt, pepper and, usually, a dash of nutmeg are added, and then the liqueur, if used.

Now the fondue is transferred to a *round* casserole (the Swiss use an earthenware casserole called a "caquelon") which has been well rubbed with garlic, and set over a warmer which may be fueled with alcohol, canned heat (Sterno), or butane gas. (Do not use a candle because it may not give off enough heat to keep the fondue bubbling as it must do.)

If the fondue gets too thick a little wine may be stirred in, but it must be warmed first. If it separates or gets lumpy, put it back on the stove and stir in ½ teaspoon cornstarch blended with a little warm wine, then stir with a wire whisk until smooth. This happens when the cheese used has not aged long enough, or when cooking and stirring are carelessly done.

The fondue is placed in the middle of the table and four or five people spear bread chunks on fondue forks or long skewers and, one at a time, dunk the bread with a figure eight stir. This keeps the fondue stirred as it bubbles.

Toward the end a rich brown crust will form on the bottom of the caquelon and this is considered a great delicacy. It can be divided among the participants or awarded to those who have not dropped any bread into the fondue!

The recipes that follow may seem similar, but each differs from the others slightly, in ingredients, amounts or method. Try them all, eventually, selecting the one you like best as a starter.

(Most of these recipes assume the use of one casserole throughout. Unless you have a round casserole that can be set over direct heat on the stove, [such as one made of Pyroceram, for example] start in another round pot made of metal and transfer the mixture to the casserole when ready to set over the warmer. In this case, rub the casserole, not the pot with garlic.)

TRADITIONAL CHEESE FONDUES

Cheese Fondue I

1 ½ pounds Emmentaler, shredded	Pinch white pepper
	Dash nutmeg
4 tablespoons flour	2 tablespoons kirsch,
3 cups dry white wine	brandy or cognac
2 garlic cloves, peeled and split	Bite-size pieces of French bread
½ teaspoon salt	

Dredge cheese with flour. Set wine over low heat. When air bubbles rise to surface (never let wine reach the boiling point) stir with silver fork. Add cheese little by little; keep stirring. Be sure each lot is melted before adding more. Keep stirring until mixture is bubbling lightly. Set a round earthenware 2-quart casserole on heating unit. Rub bottom and sides with garlic cloves. Add seasonings and kirsch to cheese mixture; blend well; pour into casserole. Spear bread on fondue fork, securing points of fork in crust. Dunk with stirring motion. Keep mixture bubbling lightly. Keep stirring as bread is speared and dunked. *Makes 6 to 8 servings.*

Cheese Fondue II

½ pound Emmentaler and
  ½ pound Gruyère,
  shredded or diced
3 tablespoons flour
1 garlic clove
2 cups dry white wine
1 tablespoon lemon juice
  (if wine is not tart
  enough)

3 tablespoons kirsch
  (optional)
Dash of nutmeg
2 loaves French bread,
  cut in cubes,
  crust on each side

Dredge cheese with flour. Rub the cooking pot with garlic; pour in the wine; set over moderate heat. When air bubbles rise, add lemon juice. Add cheese by handfuls, stirring constantly with a wooden fork or spoon until the cheese is melted. Add the kirsch and nutmeg, stirring until blended. Keep bubbling hot over burner while serving. Dunk bread and swirl in the fondue. *Makes 4 to 6 servings.*

Swiss Fondue I (TL)

1 garlic clove
2 cups dry white
  wine
1 pound Swiss cheese *or*
  ½ pound Swiss and ½
  pound natural
  Gruyère, coarsely
  shredded (4 cups)

2 tablespoons cornstarch
Salt and pepper
  to taste
Dash of nutmeg
2 tablespoons kirsch
Bite-size pieces of
  French bread

Rub garlic over inside of fondue pot. Pour in wine; adjust heat regulator to very low flame. Combine shredded cheese with cornstarch. When air bubbles rise to the surface of the wine, add a small portion of the cheese-cornstarch mixture and stir constantly with a wire whisk until the cheese is melted. Continue to add cheese very gradually, stirring constantly, making sure each addition is completely melted. When cheese mixture is smooth and starts to bubble lightly, add salt, pepper, and nutmeg. Slowly pour in kirsch, stirring until blended. Spear cubes of bread and dip and stir into the cheese. *Makes 6 to 8 servings.*

Onion-Cheese Fondue:

Add 1 envelope (1 3/8 ounces) onion soup mix to wine before heating. Proceed as for Swiss Fondue I, omitting salt, pepper, and nutmeg.

Swiss Fondue II (BF)

1 garlic clove	1 tablespoon cornstarch
2 cups dry white wine	3 tablespoons kirsch
½ pound Emmentaler, finely shredded	Nutmeg or pepper or paprika
½ pound natural Gruyère cheese, finely shredded	French bread

Rub inside of earthenware fondue dish with garlic. Pour in wine; place over low heat. When bubbles slowly rise to surface, add cheese; a spoonful at a time, stirring constantly with wooden fork or spoon. Stir until all cheese is melted. Blend cornstarch and kirsch. Stir into cheese mixture. Add spice to taste. Stir until mixture is smooth and thickened. Serve bubbling, with pieces of French bread. *Makes 8 servings.*

Note:

2 cups apple juice may be substituted for wine and 2 tablespoons lemon juice used instead of 3 tablespoons kirsch, if preferred.

Swiss Cheese Fondue (Q)

1 garlic clove	2 tablespoons kirsch
2 cups dry white wine	Dash pepper
1 pound Swiss cheese,	Dash nutmeg (optional)
shredded	Waffles or French bread
1 tablespoon cornstarch	

Rub bottom and sides of earthenware casserole or chafing dish with garlic. Add wine; heat to boiling point, but do not boil. Gradually add cheese, stirring constantly with wooden spoon until cheese melts. (Cheese and wine will not be blended.) Mix together cornstarch and kirsch; add to cheese mixture, stirring constantly. Cook a few minutes until thickened and blended. Stir in pepper; sprinkle with nutmeg. To serve—place fondue over a chafing-dish flame or candle warmer. Spear each waffle piece or bread cube with fondue fork and dip into warm cheese fondue. *Makes about 3 cups.*

Blender Fondue (LL)

½ pound Gruyère cheese,	1 teaspoon nutmeg
diced	1 teaspoon pepper
2 cups dry white wine	1 garlic clove
1 pound Swiss	Bite-size pieces
cheese, diced	of French bread
1 ½ tablespoons flour	

Place Gruyère cheese in blender. Cover and blend at high speed for 20 to 30 seconds. Remove tiny cheese bits from blender. Warm the wine (do not boil). Put 2 cups of diced Swiss cheese in blender with flour, nutmeg, pepper, and garlic. Cover and blend at high speed for 20 to 30 seconds, until cheese is in tiny pieces. Keeping blender at low speed, gradually add warm wine. Add remaining Swiss cheese. Blend until smooth. Pour cheese mixture into saucepan. Add

Gruyère cheese bits. Stir over low heat until smooth and thickened, about 15 minutes. Transfer to fondue pot and serve with French bread for dipping. *Makes 8 servings.*

Cheese Fondue-Dip (LL)

½ pound Cheddar cheese	1 tablespoon prepared
½ pound Swiss cheese	mustard
2 tablespoons flour	⅛ teaspoon garlic salt
½ cup white wine	Spoon-size shredded
	wheat

Shred cheeses. Add flour and toss lightly until cheese is coated. Heat wine, mustard, and garlic salt in a saucepan over low heat (do not boil). Add the cheese gradually, stirring after each addition until the cheese is melted.

Transfer to fondue pot or chafing dish and keep warm. With fondue forks, dip spoon-size shredded wheat into the cheese mixture. *Makes 2 cups fondue-dip.*

Swiss Cheese Fondue with Milk (ND)

3 tablespoons butter	2 packages (8 ounces each)
3 tablespoons flour	process Swiss cheese,
1 teaspoon salt	shredded
¼ teaspoon pepper	2 teaspoons Worcestershire
¼ teaspoon garlic salt	sauce
Dash of nutmeg	Bite-size pieces of
3 cups milk	French bread

Melt butter in chafing dish over direct heat. Stir in flour, salt, pepper, garlic salt, and nutmeg. Add milk gradually and cook until sauce is smooth and thickened. Lower heat, add cheese by the handful, stirring until cheese is melted after each addition. Stir in Worcestershire sauce. To serve, dunk bread into the fondue, stirring until bread is evenly coated. *Makes 4 to 6 servings.*

Swiss Fondue with Grape Juice (AD)

2 cups white grape juice, divided	¾ teaspoon salt
1 garlic clove	½ teaspoon Worcestershire sauce
4 cups (1 pound) shredded aged Swiss cheese	¼ teaspoon white pepper
	¼ teaspoon freshly grated nutmeg
3 tablespoons cornstarch	1 loaf French bread

Heat 1 ¾ cups grape juice with garlic in top of double boiler until very hot. Place over boiling water. Remove garlic. Add Swiss cheese; stir constantly until cheese is melted. (At this point cheese may not be thoroughly combined with grape juice.) Combine cornstarch, salt, Worcestershire sauce, pepper and nutmeg with ¼ cup grape juice; stir into cheese mixture. (After cornstarch is added cheese will combine with grape juice for a smooth blend.) Continue heating until smooth. Serve from chafing dish or casserole over a warmer. Each person dips chunks of French bread, speared on long forks, into cheese sauce, keeping the cheese sauce stirred. *Makes 6 servings.*

Cheddar Cheese Fondue (AC)

¼ cup butter or margarine	1 ½ teaspoons Worcestershire sauce
¼ cup flour	2 cups (½ pound) shredded sharp Cheddar cheese
1 teaspoon Ac'cent	
½ teaspoon salt	
¼ teaspoon dry mustard	Bite-size pieces of pumpernickel bread
1 can (12 ounces) beer	

Melt butter in saucepan. Blend in flour, Ac'cent, salt and dry mustard. Gradually stir in beer. Add Worcestershire sauce. Cook, stirring constantly, until mixture thickens and comes to a boil. Add cheese; cook, stirring constantly, until melted. Keep warm in fondue dish. Serve with chunks of pumpernickel bread. *Makes 2 cups dip.*

26

QUICK CHEESE FONDUES

Quick Cheese Fondue I (F)

¾ cup dry white wine
1 envelope cheese
   sauce mix

1 cup grated cheese
   Swiss cheese
   French bread

Slowly stir wine into cheese sauce mix. Add cheese and cook over low heat, stirring until mixture comes to a boil and thickens. Serve in a chafing or fondue dish with chunks of French bread for dipping. *Makes about 1 cup.*

Quick Cheese Fondue II (C)

1 can (10 ¾ ounces)
   condensed Cheddar
   cheese soup

½ cup (2 ounces) cubed
   Swiss cheese
1 medium garlic clove
   French bread

In saucepan, heat soup, cheese, and garlic until cheese is melted; stir now and then. Remove garlic. Serve hot. Spear bread with fork or wooden pick and dip into fondue. *Makes 1 ½ cups.*

Zesty Fondue (H)

4 tablespoons butter
   or margarine
3 tablespoons flour
¼ teaspoon salt
¼ teaspoon paprika
2 cups milk

1 tablespoon
   Worcestershire sauce
2 cups (½ pound) grated
   American or process
   sharp cheese
   Bite-size pieces of French
   or Italian bread

Melt butter in saucepan; blend in flour, salt and paprika. Gradually blend in milk; heat slowly, stirring constantly, until thickened. Add Worcestershire sauce and cheese; continue heating, stirring occasionally, until cheese is melted and mixture is hot. To serve in true Swiss fashion, pour mixture into chafing dish; dip chunks of bread on fork in cheese mixture. *Makes 3 cups.*

CHEESE FONDUES WITH MEAT, EGGS OR SEAFOOD

Bacon and Cheese Fondue (HW)

4 slices bacon, cooked, drained and crumbled	**⅛ teaspoon pepper**
	½ cup shredded
1 can (8 ounces) tomato sauce with onions	**Cheddar cheese**
	Bite-size pieces of
⅛ teaspoon garlic salt	**French bread**

Combine bacon and tomato sauce with onions, garlic salt and pepper; simmer 5 minutes. Add cheese, stirring constantly, until melted and smooth. Keep hot in chafing dish as dip for French bread chunks. *Makes about 1 ½ cups.*

Campers' Fondue (U)

1 package (1 ½ ounces) dry cheese sauce mix	**1 large can (4 ½ ounces) deviled ham**
1 cup milk*	**Crusty bread chunks**

Combine cheese sauce mix and milk; heat according to package directions. Add deviled ham, heat several minutes more, stirring occasionally. Serve with bread chunks for dipping. *Makes about 1 ½ cups.*

*1/3 cup instant non-fat dry milk dissolved in ¾ cup water may be substituted for 1 cup milk.

28

Chili Con Carne "Fondue" (HW)

1 can (15 ounces) chili
con carne
1 can (8 ounces)
tomato sauce
1 tablespoon cornstarch

1 package (4 ounces)
shredded Cheddar
cheese
Corn chips, carrot and
celery sticks or crackers

Heat chili to boiling; add tomato sauce mixed with cornstarch. Bring to boil again, stirring. Add cheese; heat until cheese melts and mixture thickens. Keep hot in fondue pot, chafing dish or over a candle warmer. Serve as dip with corn chips, carrot and celery sticks or crackers. *Makes about 3 cups.*

Egg Fondue (P)

½ cup butter
or margarine
3 tablespoons flour
½ teaspoon salt
½ teaspoon ground pepper
2 to 2 ¼ cups milk
5 egg yolks, slightly
beaten

¾ cup grated Parmesan
cheese
Bite-size pieces of apple
sections, celery and
carrot diagonals, green
pepper strips, and French
bread

Melt butter or margarine in heavy saucepan over low heat. Add flour; stir until frothy. Add salt, pepper, and two cups of the milk all at once. Cook, stirring constantly, until thickened throughout. Pour a small amount of sauce into egg yolks, stirring constantly. Pour this egg mixture into remaining sauce, stirring over low heat until thickened, about two minutes. Add cheese. If too thick, add more milk but do not exceed one-fourth cup. Consistency should be thick enough to coat the bite-size food without dripping. *Makes about 1 quart or 8 to 10 servings.*

Ham Fondue (U)

2 large cans (4 ½ ounces each) deviled ham
½ cup condensed cream of mushroom soup
½ cup dairy sour cream
2 tablespoons sherry
French bread

Combine deviled ham and soup in top of double boiler. Heat to boiling over direct heat, stirring occasionally. Place over boiling water, stir in sour cream and sherry. Cover and heat until warm. Serve in preheated fondue dish over warmer. Serve with plenty of bite-size pieces of French bread and forks. *Makes about 2 cups.*

Sloppy Joe Fondue (LM)

½ teaspoon instant minced onion
½ teaspoon oregano or marjoram
1 cup (4 ounces) shredded American cheese
1 can (15 ¼ ounces) barbecue sauce and beef for sloppy Joes
Bite-size pieces of French bread

Stir seasonings and cheese into sloppy Joe mixture. Heat, stirring constantly until cheese melts. Serve in chafing or fondue dish or in casserole over candle warmer. *Makes 1 ¾ cups.*

Shrimp Fondue I (IS)

2 pounds shrimp, fresh or frozen *or*
1 package or bag (1 ½ pounds) peeled and deveined shrimp
1 ¼ teaspoons grated nutmeg, divided
2 cups white wine, divided
1 garlic clove
1 pound Swiss cheese, cubed
3 tablespoons cornstarch
1 teaspoon salt
½ teaspoon Worcestershire sauce
¼ teaspoon white pepper

Clean shrimp if necessary. Place shrimp in boiling water to which 1 teaspoon of nutmeg has been added. After water resumes boiling, cook shrimp 3 minutes. Drain; keep warm. Heat 1 ¾ cups of the wine and the garlic in the top of a double boiler. Remove garlic. Add Swiss cheese; stir constantly until melted. Combine cornstarch, salt, Worcestershire sauce, pepper and ¼ teaspoon nutmeg with ¼ cup wine; stir into cheese mixture. Continue stirring until smooth. Serve from fondue pot or casserole over a warmer. To serve—spear shrimp and dip in cheese sauce. *Makes 8 servings.*

Shrimp Fondue II (C)

1 **garlic clove**	2 **tablespoons**
1 **can (10 ounces) frozen**	**dry white wine**
condensed cream of	**Rye or French bread**
shrimp soup, thawed	**unsliced**
1 **cup finely-shredded**	
Swiss cheese	

Rub chafing dish or top of double boiler pan with garlic; discard garlic. Add soup and cheese. Heat until cheese melts. Stir in wine. Cut bread into 1 ½-inch squares. To serve—spear a piece of bread with a long fork and dip into hot cheese mixture. *Makes 3 to 4 servings.*

Lobster Fondue (C)

1 **can (10 ounces) frozen**	½ **cup cooked or canned**
condensed cream of	**lobster, cut-up**
shrimp soup	**Dash paprika**
½ **soup can milk**	**Dash cayenne**
½ **cup shredded**	2 **tablespoons sherry**
sharp cheese	

Combine soup and milk in a chafing dish or saucepan. Heat slowly until soup is thawed. Add cheese, lobster, paprika, and cayenne. Heat; stir often until cheese melts. Add sherry. Use as an appetizer dunk with large cubes of bread, or pour over toast slices spread with dill butter for a luncheon dish. *Makes 3 to 4 servings.*

31

Mock Cheese-Shrimp Fondue (LF)

1 can (10 ounces) frozen
  condensed cream of
  shrimp soup
½ cup milk
2 cups shredded natural
  Swiss cheese
1 tablespoon dry sherry

2 tablespoons garlic
  spread
2 tablespoons instant
  minced onion
¼ teaspoon dry mustard
  Bite-size pieces of
  French bread

Combine soup and milk. Heat until soup thaws. Add remaining ingredients. Stir until cheese melts and mixture is thoroughly heated. Serve as an appetizer in fondue or chafing dish surrounded by French bread. *Makes 2 cups.*

CHEESE FONDUES WITH VEGETABLES

Tomato Swiss Fondue (AD)

2 cups tomato juice, divided
1 garlic clove
4 cups (1 pound) shredded
  aged Swiss cheese
3 tablespoons cornstarch
¾ teaspoon salt
½ teaspoon
  Worcestershire sauce

½ teaspoon crushed
  basil leaves
¼ teaspoon white pepper
¼ teaspoon freshly
  grated nutmeg
  Bite-size pieces of
  French bread

Heat 1 ¾ cups tomato juice with garlic in top of double boiler until very hot. Place over boiling water. Remove garlic. Add Swiss cheese, a small amount at a time stirring constantly until cheese is melted. (At this point cheese may not be thoroughly combined with tomato juice.) Combine cornstarch, salt, Worcestershire sauce, basil, pepper, and nutmeg with ¼ cup tomato juice; stir into cheese mixture. (After cornstarch is added, cheese will combine with tomato juice for a smooth blend.) Continue beating until smooth. Serve from chafing dish or casserole over a warmer, with French bread.

Italian Cheese Fondue (HW)

1 can (8 ounces) tomato
  sauce with mushrooms
2 cups shredded
  Cheddar cheese
1 tablespoon flour
1 small can (6 ounces)
  evaporated milk

½ teaspoon onion salt
⅛ teaspoon garlic
  powder
⅛ teaspoon oregano
  Bread sticks or bite-size
  pieces of Italian bread

Heat tomato sauce with mushrooms to boiling, then reduce heat to simmer. Toss cheese with flour; add to tomato sauce. When cheese melts, gradually add evaporated milk and seasonings; simmer, stirring, until smooth. Keep hot and serve with bread sticks or Italian bread. *Makes about 2 cups.*

Quick Pizza Fondue (T)

1 can (1 pound) stewed
  tomatoes
½ teaspoon Tabasco
½ teaspoon salt

½ pound process
  American cheese, grated
⅓ cup diced green pepper
  Bite-size pieces of
  French bread

Combine tomatoes, Tabasco and salt in heavy saucepan. Set over low heat; bring to boil; simmer 5 minutes to blend flavors. Stir in grated cheese; cook about 1 minute or until cheese is melted. Pour into chafing dish or one that can be kept hot. Garnish with diced green pepper. Serve with French bread. *Makes 2 ½ cups.*

Refried Bean Fondue (HW)

1 can (1 pound) refried
  beans
1 can (8 ounces) tomato
  sauce with onions

1 package (4 ounces)
  shredded Cheddar cheese
½ teaspoon chili powder
¼ teaspoon garlic powder

Combine all ingredients; heat slowly, stirring until cheese melts and mixture is hot. Keep hot and serve with heated cocktail frankfurters or corn chips. *Makes about 3 cups.*

33

BAKED CHEESE FONDUES

Baked fondues are as American as blueberry pies. They were born here, in early days, and they still flourish. Well they may, because they are fine eating and need only a green vegetable or a tossed salad to round out the meal. They began as an economy dish, when bread and cheese were either made at home or bought with pennies. The recipes showed the way to use up bread that was no longer fresh and cheese that had hardened a little. Nowadays, when no food can be considered cheap, a good baked fondue is still relatively economical, and if properly prepared, superlatively good.

Bacon Fondue

8 slices whole wheat bread	Few drops Tabasco
3 tablespoons soft butter or margarine	½ teaspoon dry mustard
	1 teaspoon
8 slices (½ pound) packaged process American cheese	Worcestershire sauce
	1 can (12 ounces) beer
3 eggs, well beaten	4 slices crisp bacon,
½ teaspoon salt	crumbled

Trim crusts from bread, spread slices with butter. Fill an 8-inch square baking dish with alternate layers of bread and cheese. Combine eggs, seasonings and "still" beer, mix well. Pour over bread and cheese. Bake at 350° for 40 minutes. Just before serving, sprinkle with crumbled bacon. *Makes 4 servings.*

Baked Cheese Fondue (C)

3 eggs, separated	1 cup shredded sharp Cheddar or process cheese
1 can (10 ½ ounces) condensed cream of vegetable, celery, chicken or mushroom soup	¼ teaspoon dry mustard
	2 cups small bread cubes

34

Beat egg whites until stiff but not dry. Beat egg yolks until thick. Blend in soup, cheese, and mustard; stir in bread cubes. Fold in egg whites. Spoon into 1 ½-quart casserole. Bake at 325° for 1 hour. *Makes 4 to 6 servings.*

Bread and Cheese Puff (AC)

8 slices buttered enriched bread	1 teaspoon Ac'cent, divided
8 slices (½ pound) packaged American cheese	4 eggs, beaten
	1 quart milk
	½ teaspoon Worcestershire sauce
Salt and pepper	Dash Tabasco

Place 4 slices bread on bottom of shallow baking dish, cutting to fit. Cover bread with half the cheese; sprinkle with salt, pepper and ½ teaspoon Ac'cent. Repeat. Combine remaining ingredients; pour over bread and cheese. Bake at 350° for 40 minutes or until top is golden brown, puffed and shiny. Serve at once. *Makes 6 servings.*

Casserole Cheese Fondue (IM)

6 slices bread	2 teaspoons seasoned salt
3 tablespoons butter or margarine	¼ teaspoon garlic powder
3 tablespoons wheat germ	1 ½ cups grated sharp Cheddar cheese
6 eggs, separated	
3 cups milk	

Remove crusts from bread; spread each slice with 1 ½ teaspoons butter. Sprinkle slices with wheat germ; put together sandwich fashion. Cut each sandwich into thirds lengthwise, then in thirds crosswise. Beat egg yolks with milk, seasoned salt and garlic powder until foamy. Arrange sandwich cubes in ungreased square 2-quart baking dish. Beat egg whites until stiff and fold into egg yolk mixture. Fold in cheese. Pour over bread cubes. Bake at 325° for 50 to 60 minutes or until inserted knife comes out clean. *Makes 6 servings.*

Baked Fondue (LL)

2 cups milk	2 cups shredded
2 cups soft bread crumbs	Cheddar cheese
1 teaspoon salt	4 eggs, separated
½ teaspoon dry mustard	

Heat milk to scalding. Add bread crumbs, salt, mustard, and cheese. Cool slightly. Beat in egg yolks. Beat egg whites until stiff. Fold into cheese mixture. Turn fondue into 1 ½-quart casserole and bake at 350° for 45 minutes until puffy but firm. *Makes 4 servings.*

Cheese Delight

5 slices buttered bread, cubed	2 cups milk
¾ pound sharp Cheddar cheese, grated	½ teaspoon dry mustard
	½ teaspoon salt
	½ teaspoon pepper
4 eggs, slightly beaten	

Alternate bread cubes and cheese in 1 ½-quart casserole. Combine eggs, milk, mustard, salt and pepper. Pour over bread cubes. Let stand 1 hour. Bake at 350° for 1 hour. *Makes 6 servings.*

Cheese Fondue Sandwich (BF)

8 slices bread, crusts removed	⅓ cup dry sherry or additional milk
Margarine	¼ teaspoon salt
¼ pound sharp Cheddar cheese, sliced	Dash pepper
3 eggs	Dash paprika
1 ⅓ cups milk	Garnishes, such as olives, cherry tomatoes, parsley

Spread bread slices on both sides with margarine. Arrange 4 slices in 8-inch square glass baking dish. Arrange cheese on top. Cover with remaining bread. Combine eggs, milk, sherry, salt, pepper and paprika. Pour over sandwiches. Let stand 30 minutes. Bake at 325° until puffy, about 30 minutes. Garnish as desired. *Makes 4 servings.*

Cheese Fondue Surprise (K)

1 ¾ cups milk
2 cups soft bread cubes
1 wedge (8 ounces) sharp
  natural Cheddar
  cheese, shredded
1 teaspoon caraway seeds

½ teaspoon dry mustard
½ teaspoon salt
Dash pepper
Dash Tabasco
4 eggs, separated

Heat milk in saucepan. Add remaining ingredients except eggs; stir until cheese is melted. Remove from heat. Gradually add beaten egg yolks; cool slightly. Fold into stiffly beaten egg whites; pour into 1 ½-quart casserole. Bake at 325° for 50 minutes. *Makes 6 to 8 servings.*

Cheese Strata I (H)

12 slices dry bread
½ pound American
  cheese, thinly sliced
4 eggs, beaten
1 can (10 ½ ounces)
  condensed cream of
  celery or mushroom soup
  undiluted

1 cup milk
¼ teaspoon salt
Dash white pepper

Remove crusts from bread; arrange 6 slices on bottom of 12x7 ½x2-inch greased baking dish. Cover bread with half the cheese; repeat layers. Combine eggs and remaining ingredients; pour over bread and cheese. Let stand 15 minutes. Bake at 350° for 30 minutes or until puffed and lightly browned. *Makes 6 servings.*

Cheese Strata II (ND)

12 slices day-old bread
4 eggs, slightly beaten
2 ½ cups milk
¼ teaspoon dry mustard
1 ½ teaspoons salt
1 ½ teaspoons Worcestershire sauce

¼ teaspoon onion salt, (optional)
Dash of pepper
1 pound process or natural American cheese, sliced ⅛-inch thick

Trim crusts from bread slices and cut each slice in half. Arrange ½ the bread slices in bottom of buttered 2-quart shallow baking dish 11 ¾x7 ½x1 ¾ inches. Combine eggs, milk and seasonings. Cover bread slices with half the milk mixture. Top bread with cheese slices, reserving 4 slices cheese for top garnish. Cover cheese with remaining bread. Pour remaining milk mixture over bread. Set baking dish in pan of hot water and bake at 325°, until done, about 1 hour. Five minutes before end of baking time, top casserole with remaining cheese slices and return to oven to melt cheese. Serve plain or with grilled tomato slices. *Makes 6 servings.*

Ham and Cheese Fondue (ND)

12 slices white bread
1 large can (4 ½ ounces) deviled ham
⅓ cup chopped green pepper
¼ cup chopped onion
2 cups shredded Cheddar cheese

4 eggs, slightly beaten
2 ½ cups milk
1 ½ teaspoons salt
¼ teaspoon pepper
¼ teaspoon dry mustard

Spread 6 slices bread with deviled ham. Place in bottom of 8 ¾x13 ½x1 ¾-inch baking dish, ham side up. Top with green pepper, onion and half the cheese. Place 6 remaining slices of bread on cheese. Combine eggs, milk, salt, pepper and dry mustard. Pour over bread. Bake at 350° for 25 minutes. Sprinkle remaining cheese on top. Bake 10 minutes longer. Let stand 5 minutes before serving. *Makes 6 servings.*

38

Corn and Cheese Fondue (AR)

1 cup soft bread cubes
1 can (1 pound) cream-
style corn
1 tablespoon minced
onion
2 packages (4 ounces
each) shredded
Cheddar cheese

1 teaspoon dry mustard
½ teaspoon salt
4 eggs, well-beaten
1 cup milk
¼ cup sliced
stuffed olives

Combine bread cubes with corn, onion, cheese and seasonings. Add eggs, beaten together with the milk; stir to blend. Gently stir in olives. Pour mixture into oiled 1-quart casserole; set in pan of hot water; bake at 350° for 1 hour. *Makes 6 to 8 servings.*

Danish Cheese Fondue (T)

1 ¼ cups milk
2 tablespoons finely
chopped onion
¾ cup beer or ale
1 teaspoon salt
½ teaspoon dry mustard
⅛ teaspoon Tabasco
3 cups grated Cheddar
cheese

6 to 8 slices bread, cut into
1-inch squares (3 cups
bread squares)
4 eggs, separated
2 tablespoons melted
butter
1 tablespoon caraway
seeds

Combine milk and onion in saucepan; heat to scalding. Add beer, salt, dry mustard, Tabasco, grated cheese and 2 cups of the bread squares. Beat egg yolks until thick and lemon-colored; stir into first mixture. Beat egg whites until stiff, but not dry; fold in. Turn into a greased 1 ½-quart casserole. Toss remaining 1 cup bread squares with butter and caraway seeds and sprinkle over top of casserole. Set in pan filled with hot water to 1 inch from top of casserole. Bake, uncovered, at 325° for 1 ¼ hours, or until delicately brown and firm, or when knife inserted in center comes out clean. Serve at once. *Makes 6 to 8 servings.*

Creole Cheese Puffs (AR)

Sauce:

½ cup sliced onion	1 ½ teaspoons salt
⅓ cup diced green pepper	1/16 teaspoon cayenne
2 tablespoons butter	pepper
¼ cup flour	⅛ teaspoon powdered
2 ½ cups canned	cloves
tomatoes	1 teaspoon sugar
1 cup diced celery	

Cook onion and green pepper in butter until tender but not brown. Stir in flour. Add remaining ingredients; cover; simmer 15 minutes, stirring occasionally. Pour into casserole.

Sandwiches:

6 slices white bread	1 egg, beaten
½ pound sharp aged	½ cup milk
Cheddar cheese, grated	

Cut bread into triangular halves. Place 6 halves on the sauce and sprinkle with cheese. Soak remaining bread in egg and milk mixture and cover to make sandwiches. Bake at 325° for 20 to 30 minutes or until browned. *Makes 6 servings.*

WELSH RABBITS AND SUCH

There are other dishes made with cheese that are close relatives of the fondue but which are different enough to go under other names. All of them are suitable for serving as a main dish for Sunday night supper, for luncheon or for brunch, all of them are easier to make than traditional fondue, and all of them are delicious.

Rabbits are often made with beer or ale, rather than wine, although some are made with milk. In addition to cheese other ingredients are used—tuna, salmon, oysters, shrimp, crabmeat, chicken, turkey, dried beef, vegetables and so on.

Then there are other dishes, much like rabbits, and also named for animals—English Monkey, Blushing Bunny, and Golden Buck for example. And one with the strange name of Ring-Tum-Ditty. Why, nobody knows. Sometimes this is spelled Ringtum-Tiddy, and sometimes Ring-Tum-Diddy. It really doesn't matter! As long as we avoid "Tummy Fondiddy"! (Honest!) All of those dishes usually contain tomatoes and bread crumbs or eggs.

Welsh Rabbit

Rabbit it is—rarebit it *isn't*. There are two stories to back up this statement, both having to do with the origin of the name. You can take your choice, but please don't be misled by overzealous food writers who changed the name to rarebit. Call it what it really is—Welsh *rabbit*. Here are the stories.

1. The Clever Cook

Once upon a time a Welsh chieftain gave a banquet, serving the game his hunters had brought home from the chase. In the middle of things, he saw to his dismay that his overhungry guests had devoured all the game and were looking around for more. As unobstrusively as possible he slipped away from the great hall and went to the kitchen to consult with his cook who was wringing his hands over the dilemma. "Make something—anything—with whatever you have on hand", pleaded the chieftain. So the cook found some cheese, a dozen or more eggs, some ale, that had lost its sparkle and a few spices. Putting them all together with tender loving care, he poured the concoction over chunks of bread which had been fork-toasted over hot coals and presented it as Welsh Rabbit to the unsuspecting, presumably foreign, guests!

2. The Empty-Handed Hunter

Long years ago, Welshmen were great rabbit hunters, for meat of other kinds was scarce and expensive. Now rabbits were prolific, and so they almost never came home without one, two or more. But one day a hunter had such bad luck that he had nothing at all to show for the day's work and came home empty-handed. The cupboard was pretty bare, too, because the housewife expected a fat rabbit to put in the kettle. Nothing but cheese and a few strips of bacon! And bread, of course. Undaunted, she cut up the cheese and set it in a pan on the hearth. Next she hung the bacon strips on cranes above the pan of cheese so that the fat dripped into the melting cheese as it cooked. Chunks of bread, toasted to a turn over the coals, went on the plates; bacon-flavored cheese sauce went over the bread, and crisp rashers of bacon were placed alongside. To taunt her unsuccessful husband she called the dish "Welsh Rabbit."

Are you convinced? Let's never say "rarebit" again!

Asparagus-Corn Rabbit

1 can (10 ½ ounces)
  condensed cream of
  asparagus soup
1 cup cream-style corn
½ pound Cheddar cheese,
  grated
½ teaspoon dry mustard

½ teaspoon
  Worcestershire sauce
Dash cayenne
2 eggs, lightly beaten
Hot toast
Cut chives

42

Combine soup and corn in top of double boiler. Set over hot water. Add cheese, mustard, Worcestershire sauce and a dash of cayenne. Cook and stir until cheese is melted. Add a little of the mixture to the beaten eggs; then return to remaining mixture, folding in lightly. Cook and stir 2 minutes. Serve on hot toast with a sprinkle of cut chives. *Makes 4 servings.*

Chicken Rabbit

1 can (10 ½ ounces) condensed cream of chicken soup	¼ teaspoon Worcestershire sauce Paprika
1 cup grated American cheese	2 tablespoons wheat germ 1 cup diced cooked chicken
2 eggs, slightly beaten	
¼ teaspoon dry mustard	4 slices buttered toast

Heat soup over hot water. Add cheese; stir until melted. Pour a little of the hot mixture over eggs; return to remaining hot mixture. Add mustard, Worcestershire and a sprinkling of paprika; fold in the wheat germ, and chicken, mix well. Heat thoroughly. Serve on toast. *Makes 4 servings.*

Classic Welsh Rabbit

1 pound aged natural Cheddar cheese	2 teaspoons dry mustard
1 teaspoon butter or margarine	1 teaspoon Worcestershire sauce
1 cup beer (about), at room temperature	1 teaspoon paprika

Shred cheese coarsely or cut in small pieces. Melt butter; tip pan to coat bottom so cheese won't stick. Add cheese; as it begins to melt, gradually add beer. Stir constantly with a wooden spoon. Add seasonings and continue to stir until the cheese mixture follows the spoon around the pan. If too thick, add a little more beer. Spoon over hot toast for a main dish. Serve with fresh apple wedges as dessert. *Makes 6 to 8 servings.*

Crab Over Corn Bread (Q)

Corn Bread:

1 package (10 ounces) easy corn bread mix	**1 egg ½ cup milk**

Heat oven to 425°. Put egg and milk into bag of mix. Squeeze upper part of bag to force air out. Close top of bag by holding tightly between thumb and index finger. With bag resting on table, mix by working bag vigorously with fingers. Mix about 40 seconds or until egg is completely blended. Squeeze bag to empty batter into special aluminum foil pan contained in package. (Do not grease pan.) Bake at 425° about 20 minutes.

Crab Meat Rabbit:

1 tablespoon butter or margarine 2 tablespoons chopped green pepper 1 can (10 ½ ounces) condensed cream of mushroom soup ¼ cup tomato juice 1 teaspoon Worcestershire sauce	**½ cup milk ¾ cup grated sharp Cheddar cheese 2 packages (6 ounces each) frozen Alaska king crabmeat, thawed and broken in pieces 1 tablespoon cornstarch 2 tablespoons water**

Melt butter in large saucepan. Sauté green pepper until tender. Add soup, tomato juice, Worcestershire sauce, milk and cheese. Cook over low heat, stirring frequently until cheese is melted and sauce is smooth. Add crab meat. Combine cornstarch and water. Add to mixture. Bring to boil. Cook about 1 minute or until thickened, stirring constantly.

44

Cut corn bread in 6 pieces. Split each piece horizontally. Place on cookie sheet and toast in broiler oven until lightly browned. Spoon crab meat rabbit over toasted corn bread pieces. Serve immediately. *Makes 6 servings.*

Crab Rabbit

¼ cup minced green pepper	1 teaspoon celery salt
1 tablespoon minced onion	2 tablespoons catchup
2 tablespoons butter or margarine	1 cup grated Cheddar cheese
3 tablespoons flour	½ cup beer
½ teaspoon dry mustard	1 can (7 ounces) Alaska king crabmeat, flaked
	Toast

Cook green pepper and onion in butter 5 minutes. Add remaining ingredients, except crabmeat, stirring constantly until cheese melts. Add crabmeat. Cook over low heat. Serve on toast. *Makes 4 servings.*

Creamy Welsh Rabbit (AD)

¼ cup butter	1 teaspoon dry mustard
8 cups shredded sharp Cheddar cheese	Dash of cayenne pepper
2 teaspoons Worcestershire sauce	1 cup light cream *or* half and half
	4 eggs, slightly beaten

Melt butter in top of double boiler, over hot water. Add cheese; heat, stirring occasionally, until cheese is melted. Stir in Worcestershire sauce, mustard and cayenne pepper. Combine cream and eggs; stir into cheese. Cook until thick, stirring frequently. Serve over any of the following: toasted, buttered English muffins; buttered toast triangles; hard-cooked egg slices; broiled mushroom caps stuffed with cooked, crumbled bacon; shrimp; crabmeat; asparagus spears and/or tomato slices. *Makes 6 cups.*

45

Golden Waffle Rabbit (C)

1 can (10 ¾ ounces)
  condensed Cheddar
  cheese soup
1 can (10 ¾ ounces)
  condensed tomato soup

¼ cup milk
4 waffles
4 green pepper rings,
  thinly sliced

Stir Cheddar cheese soup until smooth. Blend in tomato soup gradually; add milk. Heat, stirring now and then. Serve over waffles; garnish with green pepper rings. *Makes 4 servings.*

Ham and Cheese Rabbit (AR)

2 tablespoons butter
¼ teaspoon salt
⅛ teaspoon pepper
⅛ teaspoon dry
  mustard
¾ teaspoon
  Worcestershire sauce

2 tablespoons flour
1 cup milk
1 cup grated sharp aged
  Cheddar cheese
1 cup cubed canned
  ham
4 waffles

Blend seasonings and flour in melted butter. Add milk gradually. Cook, stirring until thickened. Add cheese; stir vigorously until cheese is melted. Add ham. Pour over crisp waffles. *Makes 4 servings.*

Ham 'n Egg Rabbit (C)

1 can (10 ¾ ounces)
  condensed Cheddar
  cheese soup
¼ cup milk
¼ teaspoon prepared
  mustard

6 thin slices ham
6 slices buttered toast
3 hard-cooked eggs,
  sliced

Stir soup until smooth in pan; blend in milk and mustard. Heat; stir now and then. Place ham on toast; top with eggs. Pour sauce over. *Makes 6 servings.*

Egg Rabbit (C)

1 can (10 ½ ounces) condensed cream of vegetable, celery, or mushroom soup
⅓ to ½ cup milk
½ cup shredded sharp Cheddar cheese

4 hard-cooked eggs, sliced
4 slices toast
Chopped parsley, if desired

Combine soup, milk and cheese. Cook over low heat until cheese melts. Stir often. Add eggs. Serve on toast or English muffins. Garnish with parsley. *Makes 4 servings.*

Creole Rabbit (K)

4 slices bacon
½ cup chopped onion
½ cup chopped green pepper
¼ cup flour
1 cup milk
1 can (1 pound) tomatoes, drained

1 cup shredded sharp natural Cheddar cheese
1 teaspoon Worcestershire sauce
½ teaspoon salt
Toast triangles

Cook bacon until crisp. Remove from skillet; crumble. Cook onion and green pepper in remaining fat until tender; blend in flour. Stir in milk and tomatoes; cook until thickened. Add bacon, cheese, Worcestershire sauce and salt; stir until cheese is melted. Serve over toast triangles. *Makes 6 servings.*

Scotch Rabbit (LF)

2 tablespoons butter
or margarine
1 pound Cheddar cheese,
cubed
1 teaspoon seasoned salt
½ teaspoon dry mustard

Small pinch cayenne
pepper
1 teaspoon
Worcestershire sauce
½ cup milk
2 eggs, slightly beaten

Melt butter in top of double boiler. Add cheese; stir until melted. Add seasoned salt, mustard, cayenne, Worcestershire sauce and milk. Add eggs gradually, stirring constantly to prevent curdling. Cook, stirring constantly, until thickened. Serve with cubes of French bread or over toast points. *Makes 4 servings.*

Nippy Welsh Rabbit (ND)

4 cups diced, nippy
American cheese
¾ cup milk

½ teaspoon dry mustard
½ teaspoon
Worcestershire sauce

Combine all ingredients in top of double boiler. Melt over hot, not boiling water. Add salt and pepper to taste. Serve at once on crisp crackers or toast, with tomatoes and crispy bacon. *Makes 6 servings.*

Oyster Rabbit:

Add 1 cup or more drained small oysters, fresh or canned, to rabbit just before serving. Heat.

Olive and Dried Beef Rabbit

1 cup well-seasoned
medium white sauce
(p. 73)
1 cup grated American
cheese
½ teaspoon salt
¼ teaspoon dry mustard

½ teaspoon
Worcestershire sauce
½ cup sliced pitted
ripe olives
¼ cup shredded dried
beef
4 slices buttered toast

48

Heat the white sauce over hot water. Add cheese slowly; stir until melted; add the seasonings; mix well. Add olives and dried beef. Serve on toast. *Makes 4 servings.*

Mexican Rabbit (ND)

2 tablespoons butter	2 eggs, slightly beaten
3 tablespoons chopped green pepper	¾ teaspoon salt
1 teaspoon finely chopped onion	½ teaspoon dry mustard
3 tablespoons flour	Few grains cayenne
1 ½ cups milk	2 cups finely diced American cheese
2 cups cooked or canned tomatoes	

Melt butter in top of double boiler; add green pepper and onion; cook over low heat until tender but not browned. Blend in flour. Add milk slowly, stirring constantly; cook until sauce is smooth and thickened. Heat tomatoes; gradually stir tomatoes into thickened sauce. Add a little of this hot mixture to beaten eggs combined with seasonings; stir egg mixture into sauce. Place over hot water, add finely-diced cheese; cook until cheese melts, stirring to blend. Serve hot on buttered toast, cornsticks or cornbread. *Makes 6 servings.*

Quick Chicken-Ham Rabbit (C)

1 can (10 ¾ ounces) condensed Cheddar cheese soup	¼ cup milk
	Sliced cooked ham and chicken
1 can (10 ¾ ounces) condensed tomato soup	6 slices toast

In saucepan, stir cheese soup until smooth. Gradually blend in tomato soup and milk. Heat, stirring now and then; but do not boil. Place slices of ham and chicken on toast; pour on sauce. *Makes 6 servings.*

Quick Tomato-Cheese Rabbit (F)

1 envelope (1 ¼ ounces)   1 teaspoon
  cheese sauce mix   Worcestershire sauce
1 cup tomato juice

Empty envelope of cheese sauce mix into small saucepan. Gradually stir in tomato juice. Heat just to boiling, stirring constantly. Add Worcestershire sauce. Serve over toast or crackers. (If preferred, use as a dip for luncheon meat cubes or bite-size pieces of frankfurters.) *Makes 2 to 3 servings.*

Shrimp Rabbit I (K)

½ cup chopped green   1 teaspoon
  pepper   Worcestershire sauce
¼ cup margarine   ¼ teaspoon dry mustard
¼ cup flour   ¼ teaspoon paprika
2 cups milk   Dash of pepper
4 slices American   1 can (7 ounces) shrimp
  pasteurized process   6 English muffins, toasted
  cheese cut in strips

Cook green pepper in margarine until tender; blend in flour. Gradually add milk; stir until thickened. Add process cheese, Worcestershire sauce, mustard, paprika and pepper; stir until cheese is melted. Add shrimp; heat. Serve on English muffins. *Makes 6 servings.*

Shrimp Rabbit II (R)

5 tablespoons butter   ¾ cup dairy sour cream
  or margarine   1 teaspoon minced
5 slices French bread   pimiento
1 can (10 ¾ ounces)   2 cups (6 ounces) peeled
  Cheddar cheese soup   and deveined shrimp,
¼ cup milk   cooked
  Dash white pepper   1 to 2 teaspoons minced
1 tablespoon instant   fresh parsley or
  minced onion   parsley flakes.

50

Spread butter on both sides of bread; broil until both sides are crisp and golden brown. Or, pan fry bread in butter until lightly browned. Combine soup, milk, pepper, onion, sour cream, and pimiento. Stir to a smooth consistency. Add shrimp; heat slowly to just below simmering. Serve over the warm, crisp bread. Garnish with a sprinkle of parsley. *Makes 5 servings.*

Shrimp Rabbit III (AC)

½ cup butter or margarine	1 tablespoon Worcestershire sauce
½ cup flour	2 cups shredded sharp Cheddar cheese
2 teaspoons dry mustard	
1 teaspoon Ac'cent	1 pound cooked cleaned shrimp
3 cups milk	

Melt butter in saucepan over low heat. Blend in flour, dry mustard and Ac'cent. Gradually stir in milk. Add Worcestershire sauce. Cook over medium heat, stirring constantly, until mixture thickens and comes to a boil. Add cheese; stir until melted. Add shrimp; heat. Keep warm in chafing dish or warmer. Serve with Holland rusks or toast points. *Makes 6 to 8 servings.*

Tabasco Welsh Rabbit (T)

1 tablespoon butter	½ cup ale or beer
1 pound aged Cheddar or sharp processed cheese, grated or cut in small pieces	¼ teaspoon Tabasco
	½ teaspoon dry mustard
	½ teaspoon paprika
	½ teaspoon salt

Melt butter in top of double boiler or in chafing dish over hot (not boiling) water. Add cheese and as it begins to melt, gradually stir in ale or beer. Cook only until smooth and hot, stirring constantly. Mix in seasonings. Pour over hot buttered toast; serve at once. If a thinner rabbit is preferred, stir in additional ale or beer. *Makes 4 servings.*

Spicy Welsh Rabbit (F)

2 tablespoons butter
or margarine
1 pound sharp process
cheese
1 cup milk
1 teaspoon dry mustard
1 teaspoon water

1 teaspoon sugar
¼ teaspoon paprika
⅛ teaspoon cayenne
1 tablespoon
Worcestershire sauce
2 egg yolks or 1 egg,
slightly beaten

Melt butter in top of double boiler over hot water. Grate cheese, add to butter. When cheese begins to melt stir in milk, 1/3 cup at a time. While cheese is melting, combine mustard and water and allow to stand 10 minutes. Blend in seasonings. Pour a little of the hot cheese over egg yolks; then stir into cheese mixture in double boiler; stir in seasonings; continue to stir until well blended and mixture thickens. Serve on toast or crackers. *Makes 6 servings.*

Tomato Rabbit (H)

2 cans (10 ¾ ounces each)
condensed California
tomato soup, undiluted
2 cups grated American
or process sharp cheese

1 teaspoon prepared
mustard
Toast
Crisp bacon strips

Combine first 3 ingredients in top of double boiler. Heat over simmering water, stirring occasionally, until cheese is melted and mixture is hot. Serve over toast; garnish with bacon. *Makes 4 to 6 servings (approximately 3 cups).*

Party Fondue:

Serve as a fondue, in chafing dish, by dipping chunks of French or Italian bread on a fork in cheese mixture.

Tomato-Cheese Rabbit (LM)

¼ cup butter
or margarine
4 tablespoons flour
1 teaspoon salt
⅛ teaspoon pepper
½ teaspoon
Worcestershire sauce

2 cups tomato juice
1 cup grated sharp
process cheese
Crisp rusks, toast or
crackers

Melt butter, add flour, salt, pepper and Worcestershire sauce, blending thoroughly. Stir in tomato juice slowly. Cook stirring constantly, until smooth and thick. Add grated cheese; heat just until cheese melts, stirring occasionally. Serve on crisp rusks, toast or crackers. *Makes 4 servings.*

Tomato-Onion Rabbit

1 pound sharp Cheddar
cheese
4 tablespoons butter or
margarine, divided
1 ½ teaspoons salt
1 teaspoon dry mustard
Dash Tabasco

1 cup coffee cream
2 eggs, well beaten
1 Spanish or Burmuda
onion, thinly sliced
2 tomatoes
Buttered toast

Grate cheese, or cut into small pieces. Melt 2 tablespoons butter over boiling water. Add cheese; stir until melted. Add salt, mustard, Tabasco and cream, stirring constantly. Add a little of the cheese mixture to the beaten eggs; return to remaining mixture. Cook and stir over low heat about 2 minutes. Cook onion slices in 1 tablespoon butter until they are lightly browned and tender; slice tomatoes crosswise into 4 slices; cook in remaining 1 tablespoon butter about 2 minutes. Place 2 slices toast on each plate; cover toast with onions; top with tomato slices. Pour rabbit over all. *Makes 4 servings.*

Tuna Rabbit

2 cups well-seasoned
medium white sauce
(p. 73)
1 teaspoon
Worcestershire sauce
2 cups grated sharp
Cheddar cheese

1 can (6 or 7 ounces)
tuna*, drained and
flaked
Pilot crackers

Heat the white sauce over hot water; stir in the Worcestershire sauce. Add cheese; stir slowly until melted. Add tuna, mix gently, serve over crackers. *Makes 4 servings.*

*Or use 1 can (8 ounces) salmon, drained and flaked, or 1 cup diced cooked chicken or turkey, or 1 cup peeled, deveined shrimp.

Welsh Rabbit Anchovy

3 tablespoons butter
or margarine
1 tablespoon cornstarch
1 cup milk
1 pound sharp Cheddar
cheese, grated or sliced
thin

½ teaspoon salt
1 teaspoon dry mustard
Few drops Tabasco
Hot toast spread with
butter and anchovy
paste

Melt butter over hot water. Blend in cornstarch, add milk slowly, stirring constantly for 5 minutes. Add cheese and seasonings. Cook, stirring slowly, until smooth and creamy. Serve hot on anchovy toast. *Makes 6 servings.*

Blushing Bunny (F)

1 can (10 ½ ounces)
tomato soup, undiluted
½ pound process
American cheese,
grated

1 tablespoon prepared
yellow mustard
1 teaspoon
Worcestershire sauce
Dash cayenne pepper

Heat undiluted soup in saucepan over low heat. Stir in grated cheese and seasonings; stir until cheese has melted. Serve hot as a dip with chunks of French bread. *Makes 4 to 6 servings.*

Ham and Egg Sandwich with Tomato Dippy Dunk (C)

1 can (10 ¾ ounces) condensed tomato soup	1 can (2 ¼ ounces) deviled ham
½ cup water	2 hard-cooked eggs, sliced
2 tablespoons mayonnaise	8 slices toast
½ teaspoon curry powder	

Combine soup and water. Heat; stir now and then. Meanwhile, blend mayonnaise and curry powder; spread on 4 slices of toast; spread remaining toast with deviled ham; top with egg slices. Cover with toast spread with mayonnaise. Cut each sandwich into bite-size pieces (about 12). Pour soup into bowls. With fork, dunk pieces into hot soup. Provide spoons for eating remaining soup. *Makes 4 servings.*

Ring-Tum Diddy

2 tablespoons butter or margarine	1 teaspoon Worcestershire sauce
1 tablespoon flour	2 cups finely cut sharp Cheddar cheese
1 can (10 ¾ ounces) tomato soup	1 egg, beaten
1 teaspoon salt	

Melt butter over hot water. Blend in flour. Add soup, salt and Worcestershire sauce. Add cheese; stir until melted. Pour a little hot mixture on egg; return to remaining mixture. Cook and stir until thickened. Serve on toast or crisp crackers. *Makes 4 servings.*

Golden Buck

2 tablespoons butter or margarine	1 egg, slightly beaten
1 pound American cheese, broken into small pieces	½ cup milk
	½ teaspoon dry mustard
	½ teaspoon ginger
	Salt and pepper to taste

Melt butter. Set over hot water. Add half the cheese. When melted, add remaining cheese. Melt. Then add slightly beaten egg and milk, stirring constantly. Blend in mustard and ginger. Season with salt and pepper. Serve on toast or toasted crackers. *Makes 4 to 5 servings.*

Cheesy-Topped Waffles (Q)

2 cans (10 ¾ ounces each) condensed Cheddar cheese soup	1 can (1 pound) tomatoes, drained
	1 package (9 ounces) frozen waffles

Combine soup and tomatoes in medium-sized saucepan; heat thoroughly. Bake frozen waffles in toaster or oven. Top each waffle section with hot cheese-tomato sauce. *Makes 6 servings.*

English Monkey

1 cup bread crumbs	1 egg, well beaten
1 cup milk	Salt and pepper
1 tablespoon butter or margarine	Toast or crackers
1 pound Cheddar cheese, diced	

Soak bread crumbs in milk for 15 minutes. Melt butter over low heat. Set over hot water. Add cheese; stir until melted. Add soaked bread crumbs, egg, salt and freshly ground black pepper to taste, stirring with wire whisk for 2 or 3 minutes. Serve hot, over toast or crackers. *Makes 4 servings.*

Souper Meat Loaf Sandwich with Golden Mushroom Dip (C)

1 can (10 ½ ounces) condensed golden mushroom soup	8 slices toast, buttered *or* 4 club rolls, split, and buttered
½ cup water Sliced cooked meat loaf for 4 sandwiches	Catchup

Combine soup and water. Heat; stir now and then. Meanwhile, arrange meat loaf on 4 slices toast. Spread lightly with catchup; top with toast. Cut each sandwich into bite-size pieces. Pour soup into bowls. With fork, dunk pieces into hot soup. Provide spoons for eating remaining soup. *Makes 4 servings.*

Rosy Scotch Woodcock (C)

1 can (10 ¾ ounces) condensed Cheddar cheese soup	1 tablespoon white wine 4 slices toast
1 can (10 ¾ ounces) condensed tomato soup ¼ cup milk	4 slices cooked crisp bacon, coarsely crumbled

Stir cheddar cheese soup, until smooth. Blend in tomato soup and milk gradually. Heat, stirring now and then; add wine. Serve over toast; garnish each serving with crumbled bacon. *Makes 4 servings.*

Rum Tum Ditty (C)

1 can (10 ¾ ounces) condensed tomato soup	1 cup shredded sharp Cheddar cheese
¼ cup milk	3 to 4 slices toast

Combine soup, milk, and cheese. Cook over low heat; stir often until cheese is melted. Serve over toast. (If desired, garnish with hard-cooked egg slices or sardines.) *Makes 3 to 4 servings.*

Rinktum Ditty

1 can (10 ¾ ounces)
condensed tomato soup
1 tablespoon minced
onion
2 tablespoons catchup
½ pound sharp Cheddar
cheese, grated

1 egg, beaten
½ teaspoon
Worcestershire sauce
Dash Tabasco
Toast
Crisp, crumbled bacon

Heat soup, onion and catchup, over hot water. When steaming hot, add cheese slowly, stirring constantly. Add egg; blend well. Stir slowly, over low heat 5 minutes. Add Worcestershire sauce and Tabasco. Serve on toast topped with crisp crumbled bacon. *Makes 4 servings.*

Tuna and Eggs Royal (R)

2 cans (6 ½ or 7 ounces
each) tuna
¼ cup butter
or margarine
3 tablespoons flour
1 ⅓ cups light cream
1 teaspoon salt
⅛ teaspoon black
pepper

3 to 4 tablespoons
dry sherry
¾ cup shredded
Cheddar cheese
6 hard-cooked eggs,
quartered
6 English muffins
Butter or margarine
Parsley

Drain one can tuna; break into large pieces in small bowl; set aside. Melt butter in saucepan; blend in flour. Slowly stir in cream, salt and pepper. Cook and stir until sauce begins to thicken. Add sherry; continue cooking until sauce is smooth and thickened. Blend in cheese. Gently mix in quartered eggs and drained tuna chunks. Keep warm over very low heat until ready to serve. Meanwhile, split muffins. Butter each half lightly and place under broiler until golden brown or toast muffins in toaster and then butter lightly. Drain remaining can of tuna and break into chunks. Place muffin halves on platter or individual serving plates; top with chunks of tuna. Spoon creamed sauce over each muffin. Garnish with parsley; serve while hot. *Makes 6 servings.*

3. Fondue Bourguignonne

The name of this dish is completely misleading because it is not a fondue (nothing is melted) nor is it bourguignonne (it did not originate in Burgundy nor is red wine used in the making)! However it has become an especially popular dish for entertaining, calling for special equipment and strict rules of procedure.

Perhaps the most popular version is Beef Fondue Bourguignonne. Bite-size pieces of tender beef are speared on fondue forks or wooden skewers and dipped in bubbling fat. (Experts recommend vegetable oil alone or a combination of oil and clarified butter. Unclarified butter or margarine may be used but sputtering is more apt to occur. Drop a piece of bread in the fat to decrease this.) The beef is held in the fat just long enough to cook it rare, medium or well-done, as preferred (10 to 20 seconds rare, 50 seconds, well-done). Then the meat is dunked in a sauce of the eater's choice and consumed with gusto. Not more than four or five people should gather around the fondue pot, or one fork may tangle with another.

Several sauces are provided, in small bowls set around the fondue pot. Salt and pepper shakers or peppermills are needed. A selection of condiments and relishes such as mustards, catchup, chili sauce, pickle relish, chutney, prepared horseradish, pickled onions, chopped onions, meat sauces, olives, dill-relish tartar sauce and pickled mushrooms should be on the table—perhaps arranged conveniently on a lazy Susan.

Each guest is supplied a fork (sometimes two forks are provided—one for dunking and one for eating) a small plate to hold beef chunks and spoonfuls of sauces (there are special compartmented plates designed for this use) plenty of paper napkins, and a fingerbowl filled with lukewarm water and garnished with a slice of lemon or lime or a sprig of fresh mint.

The tablecloth should be washable because there are sure to be splatters and spills.

Heat the oil on the kitchen range until it is almost smoking hot, then add butter if used, stir until melted, transfer to the fondue pot and set it on its stand over a warmer; using alcohol, canned heat (Sterno) or butane gas. This is a smaller pot than the caquelon. It is made of metal and is broader at the base than at the top. Never fill it more than half full and control the heat so that the fat does not smoke.

To Clarify Butter:

Melt butter over hot water. Remove from heat. When milk solids have settled, strain through a very fine sieve or cheesecloth into a jar and cover tightly. This will keep in a refrigerator for about three weeks.

Other Types of Fondue Bourguignonne

Several different kinds of meat, poultry and fish may be cooked in this way. Tender pork (always cook well-done), lamb, chicken, turkey, shrimp, swordfish steaks or salmon steaks cut in chunks and scallops all take kindly to the hot oil dunk and are delicious.

Sauces for Fondue Bourguignonne

Innumerable sauces are suitable for serving with this type of fondue. Choose an assortment of four or five to go with the type of meat or fish you select.

Tiny bowl-like Japanese dishes are nice for individual servings of sauce unless you have compartmented fondue plates.

Serve an array of condiments and relishes in addition to sauces.

Basic Beef Fondue With Variations (HW)

1 ½ pounds beef tenderloin or top sirloin cut in ¾-inch cubes	**Vegetable oil or buttery flavor oil**
	Dipping sauces
	French rolls, sliced

Arrange meat on platter. Meanwhile, heat oil according to fondue pot manufacturer's directions or in electric skillet set at 400°; oil should be about 2-inches deep. Spear beef cubes on fondue forks until done to individual taste. Remove to plate and serve with choice of sauces and condiments and sliced French rolls. *Makes 4 to 6 main dish servings, up to 12 appetizer servings.*

Variations:

1. *Pork, lamb or ham fondue;* Cut raw pork or lamb or cooked ham into bite-size chunks. Cook as directed for beef fondue; make sure pork is completely cooked through.

2. *Variety Fondue:* Cut chicken liver in half or sweetbreads (blanched) or kidneys into bite-size cubes. Cook as directed for beef fondue.

3. *Frankfurter Fondue:* Cut regular franks into bite-size pieces or use whole cocktail weiners, cocktail smokies, Vienna sausages or other small ready-to-eat whole sausages; cook briefly as directed for beef fondue till browned and heated through.

4. *Chicken Fondue:* Cut boned chicken breasts into bite-size pieces; cook briefly as directed for beef fondue.

5. *Seafood Fondue:* Use whole peeled, cleaned raw shrimp or scallops or cubed firm-fleshed fish; cook briefly as directed for beef fondue. Do not attempt to cook meat and fish fondues in the same oil.

Beef Fondue (S)

Proten Beef: chuck, sirloin or rib-eye steak	2 cups vegetable oil
	Dipping sauces
1 cup butter	

Cut beef into ¾-inch cubes. Carefully trim off all fat and connective tissue. Place meat in bowl and refrigerate. Prepare sauces for dipping. About 20 minutes before serving, heat butter and oil together. When the mixture bubbles and begins to brown, pour it into a 2-quart fondue dish. The hot fat should not be more than 2-inches deep. Place it on the stand over heat. When fat begins to bubble again, invite each guest to spear a cube of beef with fondue fork and lower it into the hot fat. Fry 2 or 3 minutes.

Beef Fondue Bourguignonne (BF)

Corn oil	2 pounds beef tenderloin or
Margarine	boneless sirloin, cubed
	Dipping sauces

Fill the fondue pot about ½ full with a combination of corn oil and margarine (use about ½ cup margarine to every

2 cups of oil). Preheat on range, then place in fondue stand over heating element.

Fondue Bacchus (A)

2 pounds lean beef stew meat, cut into 1-inch cubes	**Unseasoned instant meat tenderizer** **Dipping sauces**

For Broth:

1 package onion soup mix	**6 whole peppercorns,**
3 cups water	**crushed**
1 cup dry red wine	**4 sprigs parsley**
½ teaspoon celery salt	**1 whole bay leaf**

In a medium saucepan, blend together onion soup mix, water and wine; bring to a boil. Add all remaining ingredients and bring to a boil again; reduce heat and simmer until liquid is reduced one half. Strain broth through a fine sieve. Pour into a fondue pot.

Before cubing, prepare all surfaces of the meat, *one side at a time,* as follows:

Thoroughly moisten the surface of the meat with water. You may either pat the water on from the faucet with your fingers or draw a wet pastry brush across the surface of the meat. Sprinkle instant meat tenderizer evenly over the entire surface of the meat. Use no salt.

To ensure penetration and retain meat juices, pierce the meat deeply and thoroughly with a kitchen fork at approximately ½-inch intervals. Meat is ready for cubing and cooking immediately.

Place meat in a bowl or on individual plates and provide a long-handled fork for each person. The fondue fork is used to spear the meat and hold it in the hot broth for 3 to 5 minutes or to desired degree of doneness.

Dip into sauces or condiments provided.

Fondue Bourguignonne (BF)

1 ½ pounds sirloin steak (or other tender beef)	2 cups hot vegetable oil Dipping sauces

Cut beef in ¾-inch cubes for guests to pick up with fondue forks and cook to desired doneness in oil kept hot over warmer. Salt and pepper can be used, if desired, but usually will not be needed because of the sauces on hand.

Savory Fondue Bourguignonne (HW)

1 can (8 ounces) tomato sauce	½ garlic clove crushed
1 tablespoon vinegar	Vegetable oil or buttery
2 teaspoons sugar	flavor oil
1 teaspoon prepared horseradish	1 ½ pounds beef tenderloin, cut in ¾-inch cubes

Combine tomato sauce, vinegar, sugar, horseradish and garlic; chill. Heat oil according to fondue pot manufacturer's directions (or heat to 400° in electric skillet); oil should be about 2-inches deep. Spear beef cubes on fondue forks or long skewers; cook until done to your liking. Dip in tomato sauce mixture for eating. *Makes 4 to 6 main dish servings, 12 appetizer servings.*

Thrifty Beef Fondue Bourguignonne (A)

2 to 2 ½ pounds boneless round, rump or packaged lean stew meat, cut into 1-inch cubes	Seasoned instant meat tenderizer Dipping sauces

Prepare all surfaces of the meat, *one side at a time,* as follows:

64

Thoroughly moisten the meat with water—you may either pat the water on from the faucet with your fingers or draw a wet pastry brush across the surface of the meat. Sprinkle instant meat tenderizer evenly over the entire surface of the meat. Use no salt.

To ensure penetration and retain meat juices, pierce deeply and thoroughly with a kitchen fork at approximately ½-inch intervals. Meat is ready for cooking immediately. (Or cover meat loosely and refrigerate until ready to cook.)

To serve, place the uncooked cubes of beef on the table in a large bowl or on individual plates (allow about 7 ounces of meat per person). Have about 2 cups hot oil in a fondue cooker in the center of the table.

Each person spears a beef cube with his fork and dips it in the hot oil to cook (about 3 to 5 minutes), leaving the fork in the meat as a handle.

Chicken Fondue (A)

3 whole broiler-fryer chicken breasts, boned	2 cups vegetable oil
Seasoned instant meat tenderizer	Dipping sauce

Remove skin from chicken breasts. Cut each breast half into 6 to 8 nuggets about 1 ½-inches square.

Thoroughly moisten surfaces of the meat with water. Sprinkle instant meat tenderizer evenly over the entire surface of the meat. Use no salt.

Place chicken cubes in bowl or on individual plates (allow about 7 ounces per person). Have about 2 cups hot oil in fondue cooker in center of table.

Each person spears a cube with his fork and dips it into the hot oil, leaving fork in meat as a handle. When meat is cooked to taste, (about 5 to 7 minutes or until well done) remove from oil. Dip into Lemon Cream Sauce (p. 72) or sauce of your choice—and eat!

Rabbit Fondue (A)

4 pounds rabbit, cut-up   Seasoned instant meat
  ready to cook, then   tenderizer
  boned and cut into nug- 2 cups vegetable oil
  gets 1 ½-inch square

Prepare all surfaces of the meat, *one side at a time,* as follows:

Thoroughly moisten surface of the meat with water. Sprinkle instant meat tenderizer evenly over entire surface of the meat. Use no salt.

To ensure penetration and retain meat juices, pierce the meat deeply and thoroughly with a kitchen fork. Meat is ready for cooking immediately.

Place meat in bowl or on individual plates (allow about 7 ounces per person). Have about 2 cups hot oil in fondue cooker in center of table.

Each person spears a cube of rabbit with his fork and dips it in the hot oil, leaving fork in meat as a handle. When meat is cooked to taste, about 5 to 7 minutes, (must be cooked well done) remove fork from oil and dip into sauce.

For Dipping Sauce: (prepare ahead)

1 small onion,   ½ cup sliced ripe olives
  finely chopped   1 can (2 ounces) mush-
1 tablespoon vegetable oil   room pieces and stems
3 tablespoons chili sauce 1 ½ cups dairy sour cream
½ cup dry white wine

Brown onion in oil. Add all remaining ingredients except sour cream. Simmer about 20 minutes. Just before serving, blend in sour cream. Use as dipping sauce for rabbit.

Variation:

Omit chili sauce and olives. Add ¼ cup cranberry jelly.

66

4. Sauces, Dips And Dunks

Bearnaise Sauce (A)

1 cup mayonnaise
8 to 10 sprigs parsley
¼ cup chopped water
   cress
2 green onions (tops
   and all)
   Salt and freshly ground
   black pepper, to taste

1 tablespoon
   Worcestershire sauce
5 to 6 tablespoons
   Bearnaise Essence (see
   below)

Combine all ingredients in blender; blend about 5 minutes.
Serve cold. *Makes about 1 ½ cups.*

Bearnaise Essence:

1 cup tarragon vinegar
1 sprig fresh tarragon
4 whole peppercorns

2 small onions, chopped
1 bay leaf

Combine all ingredients in saucepan; simmer until reduced
by half. Strain through cheesecloth; tie solids in cheesecloth
and leave in liquid until ready to use.

Barbecue Sauce (HW)

1 can (8 ounces)
tomato sauce
with onions
2 tablespoons lemon
juice
2 tablespoons brown
sugar
1 tablespoon prepared
mustard

1 tablespoon butter
or margarine
1 tablespoon
Worcestershire sauce
½ teaspoon garlic
powder

Combine all ingredients; heat to boiling, stirring. Keep hot. Serve with any meat or seafood fondue. *Makes about* 1 ¼ *cups.*

Beef Fondue Dips

1. Combine ½ pint dairy sour cream, 3 tablespoons prepared mustard, 2 tablespoons minced scallions, ⅛ teaspoon salt and a few grains coarsely ground black pepper.
2. Combine ½ cup mayonnaise, 3 tablespoons prepared horseradish and ½ cup chili sauce.
3. Combine 1 jar (8 ½ ounces) Hollandaise sauce, ½ teaspoon onion powder (not salt), 1 teaspoon wine vinegar and ⅛ teaspoon paprika.
4. Minced Bermuda or Spanish onion.

Brown Mushroom Sauce (S)

2 tablespoons butter
or margarine
2 tablespoons flour
⅔ cup consommé
1 teaspoon
Worcestershire sauce

½ cup finely chopped
mushrooms
½ cup dairy sour cream

Melt butter in a saucepan. Blend in flour. Remove from heat and gradually stir in consommé. Return to heat. Cook, stirring until thickened. Blend in Worcestershire sauce, mushrooms, and sour cream. Serve hot. *Makes 1 1/3 cups.*

California Dip (TL)

Blend 1 envelope (1 3/8 ounces) onion soup mix with 1 pint dairy sour cream.

Horseradish Dip:

Combine 1 cup California Dip with 1 tablespoon horseradish and 2 tablespoons milk. Sprinkle top with snipped parsley. *Makes 1 cup.*

Onion-Chili Dip:

Add 1 envelope (1 3/8 ounces) onion soup mix to 1 ½ cups boiling water. Partially cover and cook 10 minutes. Gradually add 3 tablespoons flour mixed with ½ cup water. Cook, stirring constantly, until thickened. Divide sauce in half; stir ¼ cup chili sauce into one part. Serve hot. *Makes 1 ¼ cups.*

Onion-Chutney Sauce:

Into remaining onion sauce, stir ¼ cup chopped chutney. Serve hot. *Makes 1 ¼ cups.*

Mustard Dip:

Combine 1 cup California Dip with 2 teaspoons prepared mustard and 2 tablespoons milk. Sprinkle top with paprika. *Makes 1 cup.*

Ceylon Sauce (HW)

1 can (8 ounces)
tomato sauce with
onions
¼ cup chopped chutney

1 teaspoon
Worcestershire sauce
½ teaspoon salt

Heat all ingredients together. Keep hot. Serve with beef or pork fondue. *Makes about 1 ¼ cups.*

Chili Con Queso (T)
(Chili and Cheese Dip)

½ cup minced onion
2 tablespoons butter
or margarine
1 can (8 ounces)
tomato sauce
1 can (4 ounces) green
chili, chopped

1 teaspoon salt
½ teaspoon Tabasco (or
more, to taste)
1 cup large curd cottage
cheese
½ pound sharp Cheddar
cheese, grated

Cook onion in butter until tender but not brown. Add tomato sauce, chopped chili and salt. Simmer 10 minutes. Stir in Tabasco, cottage cheese and grated Cheddar cheese; cook slowly until Cheddar cheese melts. Serve warm as dip for raw carrot sticks, cauliflowerettes, cucumber slices, pepper strips and cherry tomatoes or tomato wedges. *Makes 3 cups.*

Deviled Cheese Sauce (HW)

2 cups shredded Cheddar
cheese
1 can (8 ounces)
tomato sauce

2 tablespoons prepared
mustard
2 teaspoons
Worcestershire sauce

Combine all ingredients; heat, stirring, until cheese melts and mixture is smooth. Keep hot. Serve with shrimp, chicken or frankfurter fondue. *Makes about 1 ½ cups.*

Gentleman's Choice (S)

1 cup mayonnaise
2 teaspoons lemon juice
2 tablespoons
   horseradish-mustard

2 teaspoons minced
   onion

Combine all ingredients. Spoon into serving bowl. Chill.
Makes about 1 cup.

Green Goddess Dip (S)

2 packages (3 ounces)
   each) cream cheese
2 tablespoons milk
½ cup finely chopped
   cucumber

1 teaspoon finely
   chopped onion
½ teaspoon salt
¼ teaspoon ground cumin

Allow cream cheese to soften at room temperature. Blend in
milk. Combine with remaining ingredients. Spoon into serving
bowl. *Makes 1 1/3 cups.*

Hot Cheese Dip (ND)

2 tablespoons finely minced
   onion
1 tablespoon butter
1 teaspoon mayonnaise
½ cup tomato juice
2 cups shredded
   process American cheese

2 cans (2 ¼ ounces each)
   deviled ham
Dash Tabasco
Bread sticks

Sauté onion in butter in top of double boiler over direct
heat until onion is transparent but not brown. Set over boiling water; add remaining ingredients. Stir until cheese is
melted and ingredients are well blended. Transfer to chafing dish or heat-proof casserole over candle warmer. To serve,
swirl bread sticks in mixture until lightly coated. (Add more
tomato juice if dip becomes too thick.) *Makes 2 cups.*

Hot Chili Dip (AC)

¼ cup butter
or margarine
1 medium onion,
chopped
1 green pepper,
chopped
¼ cup flour
1 can (1 pound)
tomatoes

1 can (15 ounces)
red kidney beans,
drained
1 teaspoon Ac'cent
¾ teaspoon salt
2 teaspoons chili powder
Shredded Cheddar
cheese
Tostada or corn chips

Heat butter in saucepan over medium heat. Add onion and green pepper; cook until tender but not brown. Blend in flour. Stir in tomatoes. Add kidney beans and remaining ingredients. Cook, stirring constantly, until mixture thickens and comes to a boil. Reduce heat; simmer, stirring frequently, 5 to 10 minutes. To serve, spoon into individual dishes, sprinkle with shredded sharp Cheddar cheese. Serve with tostada or corn chips. *Makes approximately 1 ½ quarts; 8-12 servings.*

Lemon Cream Sauce (A)

¼ cup butter
or margarine
¼ cup flour
1 teaspoon onion salt
½ teaspoon paprika
1 cup water
2 chicken bouillon
cubes

½ cup whipping cream
1 tablespoon lemon
juice
1 teaspoon chopped
parsley

Melt butter or margarine in saucepan. Blend in flour; brown to a golden color and add onion salt and paprika. Gradually add water and bouillon cubes; cook, stirring constantly, until mixture thickens and comes to a boil. Remove from heat; add whipping cream; heat to serving temperature. Remove from heat; stir in lemon juice and parsley. *Makes about 1 ¾ cups.*

Hot Sauce (HW)

1 jar (5 ounces) pimiento
cheese spread
1 can (8 ounces) tomato
sauce

1 tablespoon prepared
mustard
Dash Tabasco sauce

Melt cheese spread over hot water; add tomato sauce and seasonings. Heat, stirring until blended. Keep hot in chafing dish. Serve with frankfurter fondue. *Makes about 1 ½ cups.*

Italian Sauce (HW)

1 can (8 ounces) tomato
sauce with cheese
1 tablespoon freshly
ground black pepper

½ teaspoon oregano
½ teaspoon garlic salt

Combine all ingredients; simmer 15 minutes, stirring often. Keep hot. Serve with any meat or seafood fondue. *Makes about 1 cup.*

Medium White Sauce

4 tablespoons butter
or margarine
4 tablespoons flour
1 teaspoon salt

¼ teaspoon paprika
⅛ teaspoon pepper
2 cups milk

Melt butter; blend in flour, salt, paprika and pepper. Add milk all at once. Cook and stir over low heat until smooth and thickened. Cover; cook 10 minutes longer, stirring occasionally. *Makes 2 cups.*

Oriental Sauce (HW)

1 can (8 ounces)
  tomato sauce with
  mushrooms
¼ cup soy sauce
¼ cup orange
  marmalade
2 tablespoons lemon
  juice

1 tablespoon finely
  chopped crystallized
  ginger or ¼ teaspoon
  ground ginger
⅛ teaspoon garlic
  powder

Combine all ingredients; simmer 5 minutes. Keep hot. Serve with seafood, beef, lamb, pork or ham fondue. *Makes about 1 ½ cups.*

Peppery Tomato Sauce (HW)

1 can (8 ounces) tomato
  sauce
1 carrot, pared and
  grated
1 tablespoon butter
  or margarine

1 ½ teaspoons vinegar
1 ½ teaspoons sugar
1 teaspoon
  Worcestershire sauce
¼ teaspoon Tabasco

Combine all ingredients; simmer 5 minutes to blend flavors, stirring often. Keep hot. Serve with any meat or seafood fondue. *Makes about 1 ¼ cups.*

Pink Horseradish Sauce (HW)

1 can (8 ounces) tomato
  sauce
1 cup dairy sour cream

1 tablespoon prepared
  horseradish
Salt and pepper

Slowly fold tomato sauce into sour cream. Add horseradish; season to taste with salt and pepper. Serve chilled or warm in chafing dish being careful not to boil. For beef fondue. *Makes 2 cups.*

74

Sweet and Sour Sauce (HW)

¾ cup finely chopped onion	1 can (8 ounces) tomato sauce
¼ cup finely chopped green pepper	2 tablespoons orange marmalade
2 tablespoons vegetable oil	2 tablespoons vinegar
1 tablespoon cornstarch	½ teaspoon powdered ginger
½ cup water	

Cook onion and green pepper in oil over medium heat until tender. Blend cornstarch with water; add with remaining ingredients. Simmer 5 to 10 minutes. Keep hot. Serve with pork, ham, lamb or chicken fondue. *Makes about 1 ¾ cups.*

Plum Sauce (A)

Blend 1 cup plum jam and ½ cup vinegar. Serve with hot mustard on the side. (Note: Guava or apricot jam or any other tart jam can be substituted for the plum jam.) *Makes about 1 ½ cups.*

Spicy Apple-Tomato Sauce (HW)

1 can (8 ½ ounces) apple sauce	½ teaspoon allspice
1 can (8 ounces) tomato sauce	¼ teaspoon ground cloves
¼ cup firmly packed dark brown sugar	⅛ teaspoon Tabasco sauce
1 tablespoon butter or margarine	

Combine all ingredients; simmer, stirring frequently, about 15 minutes. Keep hot. Serve with pork or ham fondue. *Makes about 2 cups.*

Sour Cream Curry Sauce (S)

1 cup dairy sour cream	1 teaspoon prepared horseradish*
½ to 1 teaspoon curry powder*	¼ teaspoon salt
	Paprika

Blend all ingredients together except paprika. Chill. Place in small serving bowl and sprinkle lightly with paprika. *Makes 1 cup.*

*Amount of curry and horseradish depends on strength and individual taste.

Spicy Island Sauce (HW)

1 can (8 ½ ounces) crushed pineapple, *undrained*	2 tablespoons vinegar
	1 tablespoon soy sauce
1 can (8 ounces) tomato sauce	1 teaspoon prepared mustard
	⅛ teaspoon onion salt

Combine all ingredients; simmer 15 to 20 minutes, stirring occasionally. Keep hot. Serve with ham, chicken, seafood, pork or lamb fondue. *Makes about 2 cups.*

Steak Sauce (HW)

⅓ cup minced green pepper	1 package brown gravy mix
1 tablespoon butter or margarine	1 tablespoon dry white wine or vermouth, if desired
1 can (8 ounces) tomato sauce with mushrooms	

Cook green pepper in butter 3 to 5 minutes. Add tomato sauce with mushrooms and gravy mix; cook, stirring, until hot and thickened. Add wine; blend. Keep hot. Serve with beef, lamb or pork fondue. *Makes about 1 ¼ cups.*

Three Piquant Sauces (BF)

Mock Bearnaise:

Blend ½ cup mayonnaise, 1 finely chopped scallion, 1 ½ teaspoons tarragon vinegar and ⅛ teaspoon dry mustard.

Deviled Sauce:

Blend ¼ cup hot catchup, ½ teaspoon Worcestershire sauce, ¼ teaspoon chili powder, ¼ teaspoon soy sauce and ½ cup mayonnaise.

Swiss Sauce:

Blend ½ cup mayonnaise and ¼ cup coarsely grated Swiss cheese.

Western Barbecue Sauce (A)

1 **cup catchup**	2 **tablespoons brown sugar**
1 **cup water**	2 **tablespoons molasses**
¼ **cup cider vinegar**	2 **teaspoons dry mustard**
1 **tablespoon**	1 **teaspoon chili powder**
Worcestershire sauce	1 **tablespoon liquid**
1 **small onion, minced**	**smoke**
1 **small garlic clove,**	
minced	

Combine all ingredients in medium-sized saucepan; simmer over low heat 20 minutes. *Makes about 2 ½ cups.*

5. Dessert Fondues

The first Chocolate Fondue was born in New York City, but it was made with a Swiss chocolate bar called Toblerone! Eventually it travelled to Switzerland and has become immensely popular there.

Excellent chocolate fondue can be made with semi-sweet chocolate pieces, available in every market. Chocolate crunch bars and hazelnut milk chocolate bars also make interesting dessert fondues.

We even found a recipe for a low calorie chocolate fondue for dieters!

Chocolate Fondue (N)

1 package (6 ounces) semi-sweet chocolate morsels	½ cup light corn syrup 1 teaspoon vanilla Dash salt

Combine over hot (not boiling) water; stir until chocolate melts and mixture is smooth. Remove from heat; keep warm over hot water. Dip marshmallows, on wooden picks, into chocolate fondue. If desired, substitute for marshmallows—drained canned pineapple cubes, drained mandarin oranges, canned Bing (black) cherries, banana chunks, fresh apple slices, or drained canned fruits for salads, cut in chunks.

Brandied Chocolate Fondue (N)

1 package (6 ounces) semi-sweet chocolate morsels	2 tablespoons brandy
	1 ½ teaspoons instant coffee powder
1 tablespoon water	Dash cinnamon
2 tablespoons heavy cream	

Combine morsels and water in preheated warmer. Stir, over heat, until chocolate melts and mixture is smooth. Add remaining ingredients; stir until well blended. Keep warm. Serve the same as Chocolate Fondue.

Orange Chocolate Fondue:

Prepare according to Brandied Chocolate Fondue but substitute 2 tablespoons orange juice for the brandy, and omit cinnamon.

Classic Chocolate Fondue

3 bars (3 ounces each) Toblerone chocolate	½ cup cream
	2 tablespoons kirsch*

Break up the chocolate into triangular pieces. Combine all ingredients in small chafing dish, chocolate fondue pot or top of small double-boiler. Stir over direct low heat until chocolate is melted and mixture is smooth. Set over hot water to keep warm while serving. For dunking, use pieces of fruit, speared on fondue forks (apple slices, banana chunks, seedless grapes, pineapple chunks, tangerine sections, strawberries, mandarin oranges, etc.—all well-drained.), angel food torn into bite-size peices, split and halved ladyfingers, Butter Sponge Cake (p. 87) or Miniature Cream Puffs (p. 86).

*Or brandy, cognac, light dry rum, applejack or 1 tablespoon instant coffee or ¼ teaspoon each cinnamon and allspice.

Double Chocolate Fondue (G)

1 package (8 squares) semi-sweet chocolate	¾ cup milk
1 package (4 ounces) sweet cooking chocolate, broken into pieces	¼ cup sugar Dash of cinnamon

Combine ingredients in saucepan. Place over low heat, stirring occasionally until melted and completely smooth. Pour into fondue pot or small chafing dish. Keep warm while serving. If heated longer than ½ hour, add additional milk for a proper consistency. Use for dipping butter cookies, ladyfingers, slices of fresh or dried fruits, mints, marshmallows, or nuts. *Makes about 2 cups.*

For individual servings, pour into demitasse cups or small glasses and serve immediately.

Low Calorie Chocolate Fondue (CC)

½ cup skim milk	1 to 3 teaspoons instant coffee powder
2 teaspoons cornstarch	
1 egg yolk	Several cans (8 ounces) low calorie canned fruits for dipping
1 can (6 ounces) low calorie chocolate topping	

Combine skim milk, cornstarch and egg yolk. Beat until blended. Stir in chocolate topping, coffee powder and 1/3 cup juice drained from one of the fruits. Cook and stir over low heat until mixture bubbles and thickens. Approximately 74 calories per serving with fruit. *Makes 4 servings.*

Pineapple Chunks Fondue (D)

1 can (1 pound 4 ½ ounces) pineapple chunks, chilled and drained	1 ½ cups dairy sour cream 1 ½ cups light brown sugar

Half fill a large bowl with crushed ice. Place pineapple chunks on top garnished with mint leaves. Use wooden picks to dunk pineapple chunks first in sour cream, then in brown sugar. *Makes 4 to 6 servings.*

Variation:

Try it with mandarin oranges.

6. What To Serve With Fondues

Nothing to eat. There's altogether too much going on around the fondue table or tables to think of eating anything else until the fun is over. Some experts say that no cold drinks should be served with cheese fondue; just kirsch or brandy. Others advocate that the white wine used in making the fondue should be served. There seem to be no rules about drinks with Fondue Bourguignonne. With the latter, hot garlic bread could be on hand for those who wish it. Both types may be followed with green salad, dessert and hot coffee or tea. The Swiss themselves prefer tea.

Some people gild the lily by serving chocolate fondue after cheese or Bourguignonne, but it does seem a little too much. Fruit is better, we think. Cheese with it, after Bourguignonne, if you like.

Fruit salad can double as salad and dessert. Caesar salad is good after a seafood Bourguignonne, followed by fruit and cheese. Liqueurs may be served with the hot beverage, or afterward, as preferred.

Some "go with" recipes follow.

One Bowl French Bread (S)

3 to 3 ½ cups unsifted
all-purpose flour,
divided
4 teaspoons sugar
1 ½ teaspoons salt
1 package active dry
yeast

2 tablespoons softened
margarine
1 ¼ cups very hot tap
water
Corn meal
1 egg white, slightly
beaten
1 tablespoon cold water

Combine 1 cup flour, sugar, salt and undissolved dry yeast in a large bowl. Mix thoroughly. Add softened margarine. Add very hot tap water, gradually to dry ingredients; beat 2 minutes at medium speed of electric mixer, scraping bowl occasionally. Add 1 cup flour, or enough flour to make a thick batter. Beat at high speed for 2 minutes, scraping bowl occasionally. Stir in enough additional flour to make a soft dough. Cover bowl tightly with plastic wrap; let rest for 45 minutes. Stir dough down; turn out on to a heavily-floured board. With floured hands mold into an oblong, 15-inches long. Taper ends. Carefully place on a greased baking sheet sprinkled with corn meal. Cover; let rise in a warm place, free from draft, until doubled in bulk, about 40 minutes. Make 5 diagonal cuts on top of loaf with a sharp knife. Bake at 400° for 25 minutes. Brush loaf with combined beaten egg white and cold water. Return to oven; bake 15 minutes longer, or until done. Remove from baking sheet, place on wire rack to cool. *Makes 1 large loaf.*

Dinner Roll Variation:

Divide dough into 16 equal pieces. Form each piece into a smooth ball. Place about 3-inches apart on greased baking sheets which have been sprinkled with corn meal. Cover; let rise in a warm place, free from draft, until doubled in bulk, about 40 minutes. Slit tops with a sharp knife criss-cross fashion. Bake at 400° for 15 minutes. Brush rolls with a combination of 1 egg white, slightly beaten and 1 tablespoon cold water. If desired, sprinkle with poppy, caraway, or toasted sesame seeds. Return to oven; bake 10 minutes longer, or until done. Remove from baking sheets; place on wire racks to cool.

French Herb Bread (ST)

6 ½ to 7 ½ cups unsifted all-purpose flour, divided
1 tablespoon salt
1 tablespoon rosemary leaves
2 packages active dry yeast
1 tablespoon softened margarine
2 ½ cups very hot tap water
1 egg white
1 tablespoon cold water

Combine 2 1/3 cups flour, salt, rosemary leaves and undissolved dry yeast in large bowl. Mix thoroughly. Add softened margarine. Add very hot tap water gradually to dry ingredients; beat for 2 minutes at medium speed of electric mixer, scraping bowl occasionally. Add 1 cup flour, or enough to make a thick batter. Beat at high speed for 2 minutes, scraping bowl occasionally. *Stir in* enough additional flour to make a soft dough (dough will be sticky). Place in greased bowl, turning to grease top. Cover; let rise in warm place, free from draft, until doubled in bulk, about 1 hour. Punch dough down; turn out onto well-floured board. Divide into 6 equal pieces. Roll each piece to a rope, 18-inches long. Using 3 ropes, form a braid. Place on greased baking sheet. Repeat with remaining 3 ropes. Cover; let rise in warm place, free from draft, until doubled in bulk, about 1 hour. Bake at 450° for 25 minutes. Combine egg white and 1 tablespoon cold water. Remove from oven and brush with egg white mixture. Return to oven; bake 5 minutes longer, or until done. Remove from baking sheets and place on wire racks to cool. *Makes 2 loaves.*

Oatmeal French Bread (Q)

1 package active dry
yeast
¼ cup warm water
(105°-115°)
¾ cup hot water
1 tablespoon sugar
2 tablespoons
shortening

1 ¼ teaspoons salt
3 to 3 ¼ cups sifted all-
purpose flour, divided
1 egg
1 cup rolled oats (quick
or old fashioned,
uncooked)
Corn meal

Sprinkle yeast in warm water. Let stand 5 minutes. Stir to blend. Pour hot water over sugar, shortening and salt. Stir until shortening melts. Cool to lukewarm. Beat in 1 cup flour and egg. Add softened yeast and oats. Stir in enough more flour to make a soft dough. Turn out on lightly floured board or canvas; knead until smooth and satiny, about 10 minutes. Round dough into ball. Cover and let rest 10 minutes. To shape, roll dough to form a loaf about 15-inches long. Taper ends of loaf. Place on a lightly-greased cookie sheet sprinkled with *corn meal*. Make diagonal slits on loaf. Brush with *ice water*. Cover and let rise until nearly double .in size (about 1 hour). Bake at 400° for 15 minutes. Brush with *water* once again; reduce temperature to 350° bake 30 minutes longer. (Place a pan of water on bottom rack of oven during baking to make loaf crusty.) Cool. Cut into cubes for dipping into fondue. *Makes 1 loaf.*

Waffles (Q)

1 cup buttermilk pancake
mix
1 cup milk

1 egg
2 tablespoons melted or
liquid shortening

Place mix, milk, egg and shortening in bowl. Beat with rotary beater until batter is fairly smooth. Bake in hot waffle iron until steaming stops. Cut each waffle section into small pieces for dipping into fondue. *Makes six 4-inch waffle sections.*

85

Rapidmix Finger Rolls (ST)

5 ½ to 6 cups unsifted
    all-purpose flour,
    divided
½ cup sugar
1 tablespoon salt
2 packages active dry
    yeast

1 ½ cups water
3 tablespoons margarine
1 egg (at room
    temperature)
1 egg, slightly beaten

Combine 2 cups flour, sugar, salt and undissolved active dry yeast in a large bowl. Mix thoroughly. Combine water and margarine in a saucepan. Heat over low heat until liquid is warm. (Margarine does not need to melt.) Gradually add to dry ingredients and beat for 2 minutes at medium speed of electric mixer, scraping bowl occasionally. Add room-temperature egg and ¾ cup flour, or enough flour to make a thick batter. Beat on high speed for 2 minutes, scraping bowl occasionally. Stir in enough additional flour to make a stiff batter. Cover bowl tightly with aluminum foil. Refrigerate at least 2 hours. Dough may be kept in refrigerator up to 3 days.

Punch dough down; turn out on lightly-floured board. Divide dough into 3 equal pieces. Divide each piece into 10 equal pieces. Shape each piece into an oblong, about 4-inches long. Place in 3 greased 8-inch square pans. Cover; let rise in a warm place, free from draft, until doubled in bulk, about 1 hour.

Carefully brush dough with beaten egg. Bake at 375° about 20 minutes, or until done. Remove from pans; cool on wire racks. *Makes 2 ½ dozen rolls.*

Miniature Cream Puff Shells

1 cup water
½ cup butter
    or margarine

1 cup all-purpose flour
Few grains salt
4 eggs

Combine water and butter in saucepan. Heat to rolling boil. Mix flour and salt; stir in all at once. Stir over low heat until mixture leaves sides of pan and forms a smooth compact mass (about 1 minute). Remove from heat. Add eggs, one at a time, beating vigorously after each addition. Beat until smooth and velvety. Drop by scant teaspoonfuls* on ungreased baking sheets. Bake at 425° for about 15 minutes, or until brown and puffed. Remove from pan; cool. *Makes 90 to 100.*

*To make regular size cream puff shells for another use, drop mixture by tablespoonfuls. Bake at 400° for 35 minutes.

Pickled Mushrooms (BB)

2 cans (6 ounces each) broiled mushroom crowns	1 cup brown sugar
	2 teaspoons pickling spices
1 cup cider vinegar	

Drain mushrooms, reserving broth; place in glass jar with tight-fitting lid. Combine remaining ingredients; add ½ cup mushroom broth. Bring to boil; simmer 5 minutes; pour over mushrooms; cover tightly; cool. Refrigerate 24 hours or more before serving. Serve as a relish. *Makes about 40 pickled mushrooms.*

Butter Sponge Cake

2 eggs	1 tablespoon butter or margarine
¼ teaspoon salt	
1 cup sugar	1 cup sifted all-purpose flour
1 teaspoon vanilla	
½ cup milk	1 teaspoon baking powder

Beat eggs until thick and light. Beat in salt, sugar and vanilla. Heat milk and butter to boiling point; beat in. Mix and sift flour and baking powder; beat in. Turn into greased and floured 9-inch square pan. Bake at 350° for 35 to 40 minutes. Remove from pan to rack to cool. For dunking cut in small squares.

Index

Hot cheese dip, 71
Hot chili dip, 72
Hot sauce, 73

I
Italian cheese fondue, 33
Italian sauce, 73
Italienne, fondue al', 20

L
Lamb fondue, 61
Lemon cream sauce, 72
Lobster fondue, 31
Low calorie chocolate
  fondue, 80

M
Medium white sauce, 73
Mexican rabbit, 49
Milk, Swiss cheese fondue
  with, 25
Miniature cream puff
  shells, 86
Mock bearnaise, 77
Mock cheese-shrimp
  fondue, 32
Mushrooms, pickled, 87
Mushroom sauce, brown, 68
Mustard dip, 69

N
Nippy Welsh rabbit, 48

O
Oatmeal French bread, 85
Olive and dried beef rabbit, 48
One bowl French bread, 83
Onion-cheese fondue, 23
Onion-chili dip, 69
Onion-chutney sauce, 69
Orange chocolate fondue, 79
Oriental sauce, 74
Oyster rabbit, 48

P
Party fondue, 52
Peppery tomato sauce, 74
Pickled mushrooms, 87
Pineapple chunks fondue, 81
Pink horseradish sauce, 74
Pizza fondue, quick, 33
Plum sauce, 75
Pork fondue, 61

Q
Quick cheese fondue I, 27
Quick cheese fondue II, 27
Quick cheese fondues, 27-28
Quick chicken-ham rabbit, 49
Quick pizza fondue, 33
Quick tomato-cheese rabbit, 50

R
Rabbit fondue, 66
Rapidmix finger rolls, 86
Refried bean fondue, 33
Ring-tum diddy, 55
Rinktum ditty, 58
Rosy Scotch woodcock, 57
Rum tum ditty, 57

S
Sandwiches:
  cheese fondue, 36
  ham and egg with tomato
    dippy dunk, 55
  souper meat loaf, with
    golden mushroom dip, 57
Sauces:
  barbecue, 68
  bearnaise, 67
  brown mushroom, 68
  Ceylon, 70
  deviled, 77
  deviled cheese, 70
  gentleman's choice, 71